JESUS IS COMING–
GET READY
CHRISTIAN!

JESUS IS COMING– GET READY CHRISTIAN!

by **C. S. Lovett**

M.A., B.D., D.D.

Director of Personal Christianity

author of

JESUS WANTS YOU WELL!
DEALING WITH THE DEVIL
WITNESSING MADE EASY
SOUL-WINNING MADE EASY

cover design by AL JAMISON

Published By

PERSONAL CHRISTIANITY

BALDWIN PARK, CALIFORNIA 91706

PRINTED IN THE UNITED STATES OF AMERICA

Contents

INTRODUCTION . . . **"Jesus is coming...!"** 7

CHAPTER ONE

"Come as you are" 10

CHAPTER TWO

"FEAR—Christian motivation" 26

CHAPTER THREE

"Ready to die—as you are?" 46

CHAPTER FOUR

"The Ghettos of heaven" 60

CHAPTER FIVE

"Entering the arena" 72

"NOW THEN" 94

APPENDIX

Exposition of the parables 100

A question about crowns? 121

Explanation of the Salvation package 125

Introduction

JESUS IS COMING. . .!

Some day soon a trumpet blast will rip the heavens. A flash of glory will appear in the sky! It will be the Lord coming with all those who died, believing in Him. You and I, if we're still alive at the time, will be busy with our earthly task. When we hear the sound of the trumpet, we'll look skyward. Then. . .blink. . .wham. . .we'll be IN THE AIR! Every Christian on earth will be instantly raptured to join the host in the sky (1 Thess. 4:16-17).

When that day comes, we will be face to face with Jesus. Only three people really know what He will look like in that moment—Peter, James and John. The Lord gave them a preview of His future glory:

> **"And He was transfigured before them: and His face did shine as the sun, and His raiment was white as the light. . ."** (Matt. 17:2).

It was as if the Lord wanted us to have an inkling as to what He will look like when we meet Him in the air. Writing later, John added these details:

> **"His head and His hair were white like white wool, like snow; and His eyes were like a flame of fire. . .and His face was like the sun shining in its strength"** (Rev. 1:14,16b).

When that breathtaking moment arrives, we will stand before Jesus in that glory. Our eyes will meet His. His penetrating gaze will search our souls. This could be a joyous moment or a terrifying one—depending on whether or not a person is ready for it. I'm not speaking of salvation. Only Christians will be in this crowd. I am speaking of being prepared to have your eyes meet His.

Not every Christian is going to be thrilled with that moment. Some won't be ready to look into those eyes which are "as a flame of fire." Why? They have squandered their time on earth in living for themselves or their families. They've done their own thing, rather than joining with Jesus in the Great Commission. They didn't take Him seriously when He said He was the Master and they were His servants. So they will turn their eyes away when Jesus fixes His gaze on them. The apostle John warns of this very thing:

> **"And now little children, abide in Him, that when He shall appear, we may have confidence and not shrink away from Him in shame at His coming"** (1st John 2:28 NAS).

THE LORD'S COMING—A JUDGMENT

Many feel that salvation is enough, that a Christian is not obliged to serve Christ as Lord. This is a tragic error. Salvation is free, no doubt about that. Faith alone makes one a child of God. But God does not take us out of this world when we're saved. He leaves us here to mature in His likeness and prove our faithfulness by obeying His commands. The Word is full of exhortations to Christians to prepare themselves to meet the Lord and give an accounting of their stewardship of this life on earth.

The Lord's coming is a time of reward. We all agree on that. But the rewards are NOT for believing in Him as Savior. The rewards are for the WORKS a person has done in His name and as His servant. He says so:

> **"Behold I am coming quickly, and My reward is with Me to render to every man according to what he has done"** (Rev. 22:12).

Fire is the biblical symbol for judgment. When it speaks of Jesus' eyes as a "flame of fire," it refers to His penetrating look at our works and His searching of our persons. . .in judgment. His coming, therefore is the time of our judgment. That is when we will receive our rewards. . .based on our works. If we have been faithful to the opportunities He has given us, we will receive a rich reward. If we have ignored them, wasting our time on earth, we will SUFFER LOSS (1 Cor. 3:15). Not loss of salvation, of course, but loss of reward.

Wouldn't it be great if Jesus were to say to you in that day:

> **"Well done, thou good and faithful servant; because thou hast been faithful in a few things, I will make thee ruler over many!"** (Matt. 25:21).

WHY THIS BOOK WAS WRITTEN

The startling thing about God's call—whether in death or the rapture—is that we go AS WE ARE! That's right. If we have no treasure laid up in heaven, there will be no opportunity to acquire any after we leave this life. If we are alive at the time of the rapture, our personalities are FIXED just as they are in that moment. You see, there are no make up classes in Christianity, no second chances. We have just this one life to lay up treasure and change into the likeness of Jesus. If we don't do that now, we have to stay JUST AS WE ARE at the time of the judgment.

That's a serious thing to face, isn't it?

When you have read this book and see how the Scripture seals this truth, you'll agree that TIME is your most valuable possession. Until Jesus calls you to meet Him in the air, you can still do something about changing into the likeness of the Lord. You can still lay up treasure in heaven by getting involved with Him in building His church.

This book puts you on notice. You are now alerted to the fact that ALL believers must stand before the judgment seat of Christ and give an account of their works in the flesh. Within these covers are instructions for getting ready for that moment. Since the judgment occurs when we meet the Lord in the air, let it be a warning to your soul when anyone says. . .

JESUS IS COMING!

Chapter One

COME AS YOU ARE

Ever attended a "Come as you are" party? There is a judge at the door. His job is to note each guest, checking on his appearance. A prize is awarded for the most unique or unusual costume. The judge evaluates each person, appraising every detail of his appearance. On the basis of that appraisal, the prizes are presented.

It is like that at the Lord's **come as you are** event.

When death summons the Christian, the first Person he meets is the Judge. The Judge reviews every detail of the Christian's life. He then makes an award based on His appraisal. For some this will be a pleasant experience. Others will find it threatening and uncomfortable.

Ever get a traffic ticket? Miserable feeling, isn't it? If you have to appear, it is even worse. Nobody likes that. It is uncomfortable having a judge examine you and make a decision about you. You feel almost naked. You fidget. Along with every other Christian, you will suffer personal inspection at the door of heaven. You are to have your day in court.

Am I teasing? No. This is precisely what happens when a Christian dies.

BEFORE THE JUDGE

> **"It is appointed unto men once to die, after that the judgment"** (Heb. 9:27).

I doubt if that's a surprise. It's quoted so often. We've said that death was an invitation. Now see it as a court summons. One of the clearest announcements of God's Word is the fact of our forthcoming judgment:

> **"So then each one of us must give an account of himself to God"** (Rom. 14:12).

There is no choice about this. There is no way to avoid appearing. We will keep this appointment. No one can get by the Judge:

> **"For we must all appear before the Judgment Seat of Christ, that each one may be recompensed for his works in the body, according to what he has done, whether it be good or bad"** (2 Cor. 5:10).

That doesn't startle you. The verse is familiar.

Please notice WHO appears — we do, **Christians**. It even tells **why** — to be **recompensed** or rewarded for the WORKS done while in the body. We receive something for ALL our works, whether good or BAD. Ouch! Did you get that word, **bad?** It could give one the jitters. This judgment is serious. It takes into account EVERYTHING we've done during our time on earth. We have a popular quote based on this truth:

"Only one life . . .
'Twill soon be past,
Only what's done
For Christ will last!"

This is one of the best known sayings of our time. Believers parade it everywhere. But does the hard truth of it register? Does the average Christian understand what it really means?

WHAT IT MEANS

Those words declare the lasting effect of a Christian's WORKS accomplished during his life on earth. They say ONLY what is DONE **for** Christ abides forever. That's what "will last" really means. Do you believe all you will take from this life is what you have **done for Christ?** If that quotation is true, every opportunity to do anything **lasting** ends at death. Death, then, ends all opportunity to get ready for heaven. Every chance to invest in Christ ceases at the summons. A man's last breath closes the door on his final opportunity to extract anything **eternal** from this life.

I was sharing this truth with a dear Christian friend. I wasn't ready for his reaction. He is a determined believer in the Lord Jesus and truly loves the

"You go serve Jesus all you want!"

Word. My spirit groaned when he leaned back in his chair and sighed his reply. . . . .

> "Oh, I think if a man gets to heaven that's good enough. There isn't anything required of me but keeping my faith centered in Jesus and treasuring His Word. He paid it all. As far as I'm concerned, that even takes care of all my failures in this life."

I didn't want to argue. His indifferent smile was one of total satisfaction with himself. However, I thought I'd ask a question, just to plant a thought:

"Do you believe in the Judgment Seat of Christ?"

"Sure. It's in the Word." He was proud of that assertion.

"Do you believe it to be a time of judgment for Christians?"

"Yes."

"Well, if it doesn't matter what we do with our lives on earth and all Christians are treated the same, why is there a judgement at all? What would be the point of such a judgment?"

He didn't reply.

Of course, I wasn't challenging the fact that "Jesus paid it all." When it comes to salvation, I too, insist His precious blood makes us whiter than snow. A sinner can no more make himself righteous than a brain surgeon can operate on his own brain. But that wasn't the point. I wasn't speaking of salvation. I was asking my friend why blood-bought, blood-washed saints **had to appear** at this judgment? Why do the redeemed **account** for deeds done in the body?

What kind of a judgment metes compensation to Christians for both EVIL and GOOD works? On what basis? If it doesn't matter what a Christian does with his life, why does he have to appear? Does the blood of Christ finally make this judgment a joke?

THE JUDGMENT A JOKE?

Could the idea of ONLY ONE LIFE be nothing more than a poem? And what the Word calls the Judgment Seat of Christ merely a time when God shows His people how childish, foolish and helpless they are? What should we think of the weight of Scripture which testifies to the awfulness and solemnity of that day in court? It can't be a joke. Does God mean to mock those for whom He died? Hardly. But neither are we to mock Him with wasted lives:

> **"Be not deceived, God is not mocked; for whatsoever a man soweth, that shall he also reap"** (Gal. 6:7).

The Apostle delivered those penetrating words to Christians. There is nothing humorous about them. This matter is far from a joke. Look at that word... **"deceived."** Who would deceive us about something as serious as judgment? God? Never. Only Satan. How? By making us think that the blood of Christ somehow CANCELS the law of the harvest; that Christians will NOT reap what they sow.

Deceived, you say?

Anytime we think we can mock God with a wasted and selfish life, especially after He has made such a huge investment in us, we have to be deceived. The Lord is after disciples. He wants people as eager to invest in Him, as He is to invest in them. All are clearly told what He expects of them. A fruitful life will reap a joyous harvest in eternity, a wasted life will reap the bitterness of LOSS. Anyone who feels God overlooks disobedience and indifference to His commands has to be deceived.

As I watched that satisfied smile stretch satanically across my brother's face, I was sick in spirit. I knew Satan had put it there. Poor beloved child of God, the devil had gotten to him with a wile. What wile? The one which suggests that everything we ever hope to HAVE or BE is automatically included in the salvation package.

Exaggerated salvation — a dangerous wile.

We think of ourselves as redeemed. We are also **bought**. The Lord paid the price "of His own blood." That made us His personal property, His slaves. If that word is uncomfortable, I will say that we are His servants. Later, I mean for us to get used to the word, SLAVE. Being a slave of Jesus isn't as bad as it sounds. True, few know anything about serving Him as Master, but if this book does what it is supposed to, that will change.

The satanic wile which exaggerates salvation to the place where Christians feel no obligation to Jesus, is dangerous. And because sonship in Christ is so full and free, it is easy for the devil to stretch it to include everything else. Some have even said, **"There is nothing anyone can do for God."** Satan gleefully rubs his hands when Christians talk like that. Anyone believing it will never submit himself as a servant of the Lord.

● The salvation package is BIG, no question about that. There are amazing rights and privileges which come with it. But privileges don't wipe out responsibilities. We have rights in Christ, but we also have a stewardship. Rights do not repeal our obligation. Having Jesus as Saviour does not revoke the requirement to serve Him as Lord. Jesus is both Saviour and Lord. We are both servants and sons. **Sonship** in the family of God does not abolish **service** to Christ. Yet Satan would have us think so.

A man becomes a child of God through faith in the Lord Jesus — **period**. But the KIND OF A CHILD he is, depends on the Christian. He can make of himself whatever he desires. He can be as fully like Christ as he desires, or as little. The same is true of wealth laid up in heaven. A man can be as rich in the Lord as he wants, or he can be poor. He will still be in heaven. What Satan hides, is the fact that what we **become,** and what we **have** in the Lord is **up to us**. He would have Christians believe **everything** is included in the salvation package. But it isn't.

● Neither does it cancel the law of the harvest. We do REAP what we sow, child of God or not. If we fail to live for Christ, we will suffer the consequences. If we refuse to press for a holy life, we will be sorry. While the blood of Christ clears us from the GUILT of sin, it does NOT REMOVE the consequences. When the Word says we reap what we sow, it is speaking of consequences, **not guilt**. There is a big difference.

THE DIFFERENCE

Sin brings guilt and consequences. Jesus bore the guilt at Calvary, but we retain the consequences. His work on the cross does NOT cancel the **results** of sin. Are we not forgiven? Yes, totally and completely. But what is forgiven? Guilt, that's **all** one can forgive. **You can't forgive consequences**. Let me illustrate.

You give your son a new bicycle. He begs to ride it to school. You consent after he promises to lock it to the bike stand. But he forgets. When school is out he finds his bike is gone — stolen! He returns home crying. Out comes his story. He's sorry he didn't lock the bike as promised. He asks your forgiveness. You show mercy.....

"That's all right son, I forgive you."

There, isn't that nice? He's totally forgiven. He escapes your wrath. There is no punishment. He relaxes. Hey! Wait a minute. Something's wrong here. **Where's his bicycle?** Gone! He's forgiven, but he has no bike. Alas, the **consequences remain.** He is forgiven, yet he reaps the harvest of his disobedience. Your forgiveness did not bring back his bicycle.

The blood of Christ removes the GUILT of our sin. We are not punished, because we are no longer guilty. But the blood **does not** cancel the consequences anymore than forgiveness could restore the boy's bicycle. His guilt was gone, but so was his bike. **Guilt has to do with punishment.**

Consider the man who carelessly kills his wife. He didn't mean to. He is brought to trial. The jury finds him NOT GUILTY. He did kill her, but now there is no guilt. And because there is no guilt, there is no punishment. Did the jury's verdict bring his wife back? No, she's gone. The consequences remain. Forgiveness by the court did not restore his wife.

And so with us. Jesus' blood applied to our souls means NOT GUILTY. It does not mean that we have never sinned, only that we are no longer guilty of it. It is as though we had not sinned **as far as punishment is concerned,** but the consequences remain. This book is concerned with the consequences of a wasted life. The Lord will forgive us for throwing away the opportunity of our life on earth, but His forgiveness will not replace what we lose by doing so. We will never be PUNISHED, but we will suffer loss for wasting our opportunities in Christ.

It is with GUILT GONE that we stand before the Judgment Seat of Christ. Hence we know it is **not** for sin. The guilt of sin would have taken us to another court. . . .the GREAT WHITE THRONE (Rev. 20:11). So it is as **forgiven people** we appear. The Judge looks us over. He examines what we have done, He evaluates our persons. His appraisal determines the CONSEQUENCES of our lives on earth. Satan says there are no consequences, that the salvation package takes care of all failures in the Christian life. Let's see if it does.

THE SALVATION PACKAGE

In saying salvation DOES NOT cancel the consequences of a wasted life, I do not mean to minimize what we **do have** in Christ. The Lord has done great things for us, but ALL are things we could NOT DO for ourselves. Anything we can do, He expects us to do. Salvation is free, but after that, **everything else** is EARNED. With the package so rich and full, it is easy for Satan to suggest it includes more than it really does. Christians listen when his suggestions magnify the Lord, and appeal to their carnal natures at the same time.

Doesn't it sound Christ-honoring to say, **"All I am, or have, or hope to be, is in Christ?"** Sure. Apart from Him we are nothing. But see how tricky that is. Those words "in Christ" can be **used deceptively**. For even our service, our stewardship, our obedience is "in Christ." The business of laying up "treasure in heaven" is also **in Christ,** so is the need to "grow up." (Eph. 4:15). But are not these things WE DO? See? By stretching the truth just a little, Satan cancels Christians who might otherwise be terrific servants of the Lord.

● It is not within the purview of this book to discuss all we have in Christ, but I must list the items in the salvation package. If first I show what it DOES include, then by contrast I can show what it DOES NOT include. That will keep our thinking straight. Here then are the seven specifics of salvation:

1. **ETERNAL LIFE**
2. **SONSHIP**
3. **RIGHTEOUSNESS**
4. **FORGIVENESS**
5. **THE HOLY SPIRIT**
6. **AUTHORITY**
7. **INHERITANCE**

A full discussion of the "Salvation Package" appears in the appendix, page 125

● The salvation package includes everything we CAN NOT do for ourselves. It is complete, providing everything Christians need to live, both on earth and in heaven. Every item in the package is GIVEN, nothing about it is EARNED.

> **"Blessed be the God and Father of our Lord Jesus Christ, Who has BLESSED (given) us with every spiritual blessing in the heavenly places in Christ"** (Eph. 1:3).

Blessings are BESTOWED, not earned. They come DOWN. They are not **sent up**. No one can "lay up" blessings in heaven. And note that we have all these right now, **as present possessions**. True, we must wait to enjoy some features such as the glorified body, but nonetheless it is ours this moment. Not one thing has been withheld. You and I have received everything God GIVES any of His children.

WHAT THE PACKAGE DOES NOT INCLUDE

There are some things God CANNOT give, things **we must** do. He can give us the package, but it is up to us what we do with it. Salvation is free. All that comes with it is free. But after that, EVERYTHING ELSE is earned. Why? There is no way for God to give it.

What is it God cannot give? For example, we know the package includes a task we are to do for Jesus, a commission. Can God give someone a job and then hand him **obedience** as a gift? No. Obedience is something a man must GIVE HIM! Can the Lord design us with the ability to MATURE in Christ, and then **hand us maturity?** Impossible. Maturity cannot be given, it must be REACHED. Can He give us total freedom so that we may do with our lives as we please and then make us a **present of faithfulness?** Never. Faithfulness cannot be given. Christians must **be** FAITHFUL to the Lord.

● See the difference? There are two sides to life in Christ. God's part and our part. There is that which God does for us, and what we are to do for Him.

Notice that difference in **direction.** What God does is **toward** us. What we do is **toward** God. God's blessings come DOWN to man, man's response GOES UP to God. Anything we can GIVE GOD is NOT in the salvation package. Granted, the ability to serve Him comes via the Holy Spirit, but **meeting our responsibility** isn't. The Indwelling Spirit enables us to discharge our obligation to God, but His presence **does not** relieve us of responsibility. To the contrary, we have even less excuse for faithlessness. God gives us the opportunity, taking advantage of it is our part.

So I took leave of my friend.......

Now you know something of what was in my mind as I said goodbye to him. I was serving Christ, thrilled with the joy it brought to my life. I wanted my friend to have it too. As I thought of the day when he would have to turn in his record, my heart went out to him. I longed to ease him into action for Jesus.

But there he sat. His hands clasped behind his head, looking on me with pity. He felt sorry for me. He was convinced I was foolishly slaving for Christ, when I could be taking my ease and enjoying the good life. He thought I was missing the best of two worlds. I could read it in his eyes, but he told me anyway....

> "Well, I'm going to keep on relaxing. Jesus has done everything for me. You can work as hard as you like, but I doubt if you'll end up any better off than I will."

What could I say? He is a gracious person, faithful to his church and devoted to God's Word. By most standards he is a superb Christian. In no way is he greedy or graspy, but kind and considerate. Nothing delights him more than a spiritual discussion with the wonders of Christ extolled. I looked at his languishing form stretched in that big chair, I thought to myself.....

"There is one man who really teases the Lord Jesus."

THE MAN WHO TEASES JESUS!

Once when the Lord was teaching in the temple at Jerusalem, some religious leaders came to interview Him. He put a parable to them:. . . . .**"What is your opinion about this:**

> There was a man with two sons. He went to the first and said, 'Go work in the vineyard today my son.' The son replied, 'all right sir,' but he never went near it. Then the Father approached the second son with the same request. He said, 'I won't.' But afterward changed his mind and did go into the field. Which of these two did the will of his father?" (Matt. 21:28-31).

The leaders replied correctly, **"the second one."** But they resented it when the Lord applied the parable to them. With all of their religious activity, they were **saying** "yes" to God, but were not **obeying** Him. On the surface they **appeared** to be His servents, yet they were **not doing** His will at all.

Ever watch an older boy tease a little child, tempting him with a toy? He holds it out as if promising to give it, but when the child reaches for it, he withdraws his hand. That's heartless you say? Even cruel? Some boys are mean enough to make a toddler cry.

But then have you wondered how God might feel about Christians who **appear** to be devoted to His will, but never get around to **doing it?** Such a thing can only be distressing, even tantalizing. To have people draw nigh to God with loud professions of faith and declarations of submission, must sound wonderful to His ears. But when they go off to live as they please, it can only bring an ache to His heart.

● You wouldn't think Christians would do that to someone as nice as Jesus, but they do. Not deliberately, perhaps, but many treat the Lord Jesus that way. When it comes to serving our Master, they just aren't interested. I can't help but think of a person who treats our precious Savior in that fashion as someone who teases Jesus. You know the kind I mean. Say, I think I see one now. Let's see what he is up to.

Follow that man. . . . . .

There he goes. That's Mr. American Christian on his way to church. He is saying "yes" to the Lord. Why else would he bother to go to church? Ah, he sounds like an evangelical. Listen to him at testimony time. He's telling everyone how glad he is to be in Christ. Proudly he says his sins are washed away by the precious blood of Jesus. Yes sir, he's an evangelical. They talk like that. See how he stands to identify himself with Jesus — in church. It must please the Lord to see a saint so bold. This looks promising. Surely if the Master asked this man to do anything, he'd do it. But that's what we came to see.

It's time to sing. Catch that enthusiasm as he joins the tumult.

"Jesus paid it all, all to Him I owe!"

Glorious! Marvelous! No words could be truer. And my, what gusto he gives them. Here comes another song:

"I'll go where you want me to go, dear Lord;
over mountain, or plain or sea;
I'll say what you want me to say, dear Lord;
I'll be what you want me to be. . . ."

Isn't that great! Precious! This man is so eager to serve the Lord he puts his willingness to song. Wonderful. I'll bet when we follow this man from church we will really see a devoted servant in action. No one can feel that way about Christ and refuse to go all out. Shhhhhh . . . the service is ending. People are leaving now.

"Pastor, that was great! Just what I needed to hear."

I expected him to say that, didn't you? That should settle it. Our man has testified to what Jesus has done for him. Has expressed his personal commitment in song. Now he acknowledges God's minister has spoken to his heart. Surely nothing could keep this man out of the vineyard — **we hope**. Wouldn't it be awful for him to give such assent to the Lord's call on his life and then forget it? Whew! That would really tease the Lord. AH. . . .I can't believe anyone would be so cruel to Christ, can you?

I see our man isn't going directly home. He's stopping for gas. Now to see a servant in action. His vigorous faith will surely spill over on the attendant. At least he will get out of his car to leave a tract in the restroom. Anyone could do that, and not be too dedicated either. Let's watch. . . . .

"That's $4.38."

"Here you are."

"Thanks, and here are your stamps. Come again."

"I sure will. So long."

Hey, wait a minute! Didn't you forget something? He didn't say a word. All he did was get a little service for his car. Nothing was done for Jesus. This doesn't make sense.

The man who teases Jesus says nothing.

Could a man furiously avow his debt to Christ, declaring he will do anything and go anywhere for Him, leave the church and forget it. . . . .? Huuuuummmmmh, this looks suspicious.

You don't suppose our "evangelical" is all talk, do you? Perhaps he is not so devoted to the Master after all. But we should give him the benefit of the doubt. Besides one stop is not a fair appraisal. Hey, his car is pulling into a supermarket. Apparently they need a few things for dinner. Maybe this is where we will see our man in action. Markets are wonderful places to obey the Master, great places for reaching lost souls.

There he is at the magazine rack. Probably he is going to conceal a tract inside. Oh, he put it back. Well, maybe he plans to speak to the clerk over there dusting stock. He isn't too busy. Nobody's around. Wow, he passes him up. I guess he means to put a tract in the phone booth. Nope. He hands some coins to the cashier. A few words of polite exchange, but nothing for Jesus.

Do you suppose he is saving his strength to put tracts in the cars in the parking lot? His car is parked some distance away. He must pass some empty vehicles. Even if the windshield wipers are too heavy to lift, a slight toss into an open window isn't overly taxing. He can do that. Just one. . . . pleeaassee? Not even one? Awh. . . . that's too bad. Nothing for Jesus. And the opportunity is so easy and natural even a child could do it. What are we to think about that?

● If Christ is not the CENTER of a man's **routine,** He is not the center of his **life**. A man's daily routine of job, plus all the contacts and trips it takes to exist in this world. . . .is the ORBIT of his life. If Christ is not at the very heart of that routine, He is not the focal point of a Christian's life. There is no way to be a servant of the Lord and exclude Him from that routine.

When people **eat** what THEY want, **go** where THEY want, **do** what THEY want, **see** what THEY want, **say** what THEY want, **spend** THEIR money to suit their own fancy, **use** THEIR time as THEY please, **squander** THEIR talents as THEY see fit, for whom are they living? Plainly they are living for **themselves,** not for Jesus. No matter how ceremoniously they declare themselves at church, they are definitely NOT the servants of Christ. Do such Christians realize all they are and have belongs to Christ? In theory, perhaps. In action, no. Consequently they **tease** the Lord with their words, and **defy** Him with their lives.

WHEW!. . . . .

Should death find you unwilling to invest yourself for Christ, you will appear in that SAME unwillingness. You will feel NO MORE like serving Him then, than you did a split-second before. Nothing about the transition changes you. You remain the same person you were on earth. Your feelings about Christ and serving Him will be the same as well.

And that's rough.

If you do not learn to ENJOY the Lordship of Christ during your time on earth, there is nothing about the next life to make you like it any better. If you don't thrill to serving Jesus now, there is nothing about heaven to make it more appealing. Christ Jesus will be as FULLY your Lord there as He is here. Heaven will not diminish His LORDSHIP a bit. There is nothing about death to change your feelings about it.

● So how would you like to appear before Him **as you are** this minute? How would you be dressed? Would you be clothed in the JOY of serving the Lord, or would you be found PUFFED with the preference of living for yourself? Would your record show you cared most for Him or for yourself? Think about that. This is exactly what it will be like. The Judgment Seat of Christ is the crisis of Christianity!

That's what prompted me to call this book, "Why Die As You Are!" The question is valid. There's time to change. The point, dear reader, is — WILL YOU? If you fear God you will. And don't let anyone tell you it is wrong to fear the Lord. The noblest servants of any age have been God-fearing. Until a man learns to fear the Lord he is not apt to take His Word seriously. The Bible offers more than precious promises. It contains important warnings as well. A man is a fool to treasure the promises and ignore God's warnings. The fear of God is proper motivation for Christians, as we see—next.

How would you like to appear that way in heaven?

Chapter Two

F E A R — Christian Motivation

When I was seventeen, I joined the horse-mounted cavalry, spending my summers training at the Presidio of Monterey. On this particular day we had just returned from an outing. We were brushing our mounts at the picket line. Suddenly someone yelled.

"Hey! Look at that! Watch out!"

We all turned. Bearing down on us was a driverless car. It had rolled from its parking place on the hill above. In a split second we saw the danger. We scrambled. I was scared. In my desperate getaway, I jumped a 5 foot fence separating the picket line from the stables. Then the car hit.

My horse had to be destroyed. In another second I would have been a goner. When it was over I took another look at the fence. I stood there shaking my head in unbelief. I had never jumped anything that high in my life. I haven't since. Doctors explain it as adrenalin in the blood. I felt it as **fear**.

FEAR IS GOOD

Biologists tell us fear is universal, the first emotion to develop in man. You and I enter this world with **fear** installed as original equipment. It grows. As we advance in knowledge and suffer threatening experiences, our capacity to fear increases.

> "We cannot live our natural or spiritual lives without fear. A man will never be a first rate surgeon unless he learns to fear infection. A child will never be safe to leave alone until he fears to throw a lighted match into a wastepaper basket. . . ."*

*The Keswick Calendar.

The life that does not fear in this present world is an abnormal one. Fear is the **warning of danger.** It prods us to action. We can be thankful for it. Without it we would quickly run into ruin.

Get your hand too close to a hot burner — OUCH! There is pain. Instinctively you draw away from the heat. Now that is marvelous. Think of the charred, mutilated hands we'd have if it were not for this device. No one enjoys pain, but how grateful we are for its warning. Were it not for pain, our bodies could become useless in a very short time.

The soul has a similar device — **FEAR.**

WHAT PAIN IS TO THE BODY
FEAR IS TO THE SOUL!

Fear is an emotional jab to the heart. It pricks the slumbering elements of a man's mind. It makes him look up to see approaching danger. Fear has to do with what is coming — **always.** Fear and the future go together. As surely as God has designed us capable of courage, so has He placed within us the warning gong — fear. When that gong sounds, danger lies ahead. Fear sets a person for action. Many fears, of course, are physical. We're concerned with that which is spiritual.

THE FEAR OF GOD

The fear-device within our souls performs its noblest duty when it causes us to fear God. People's souls meet dangers as well as their bodies. There are spiritual dangers. They range from being outside of Christ and headed for hell, to being out of God's will and in danger of His judgment.

> **"It is a fearful thing to fall into the hands of the living God!"** (Heb. 10:31).

Few can claim to be in the center of God's perfect will. Most live on the fringes of His best. Wouldn't you hate to think that the Christianity of our day is the best God has for His people? American Christianity has no fear of God.

Of our American Pioneers it has been said, **"They feared nothing but God."** Today, the reverse is true. People **"fear everything but God."** That applies to Christians and non-christians alike. Danger lies ahead — not merely for those without Christ, but also for the servants of the Lord. Those blood-bought slaves who live indifferently to the Master's command, have something to fear.

FEAR MOVES MEN

> "Happy is the man that fearth God, who delights in His Commandments" (Psa. 112:1).

Fear does its highest work when it causes us to reverence our Lord Jesus as Master, and submit ourselves as His servants. Now there is of course, **ungodly fear**. We're not talking about that. Sinful man is filled with fears. He has so many the 365 "fear nots" of the Bible are insufficient for him. People fear people, dread things and tremble at circumstances. The answer to human fear is found inscribed on a monument to Lord Lawrence in Westminster Abbey:

> **"He feared man so little, because he feared God so much."**

That also applies to Christians. There is such a thing as godly fear. I speak of that godly fear of the Lord which can guard and guide our lives. When it stings our souls, as pain stabs the body, the fear of God can move us to right action — fast. When we move into the will of God, it brings joy to our souls. Godly fear will never stir us to do anything which will hurt our lives.

We all sense that the Lord Jesus has done so much for us we will never be able to repay Him. We respond to His love, but we don't begin to sacrifice for Him as He did for us. We hate to admit that our love doesn't motivate us as it should, but it is true. Consequently FEAR moves us to duty quicker than gratitude. But that isn't as bad as it sounds. God knows what we are. Thus His servant declared godly fear as the path of blessing:

"Blessed is everyone that feareth the Lord, that walketh in His ways" (Psa. 128:1).

It is fear, not love, that moves us to total commitment. I know you wonder about that. But God Himself placed this device in our souls. As sinners, we love ourselves. So to protect us from wasting and destroying our lives in disobedience, He has given us the capacity to fear Him. This is not brutal, it's a kindness. It does not interfere with our love for Him. It's sole purpose, as with pain in the body, is to **warn us of danger**. Can't you consider it a gift to have an alarm system within your soul which warns when you are out of God's will? That's what godly fear does. The only time it bothers is when you are in **spiritual danger**.

If it is true that......

"THE FEAR OF THE LORD IS THE BEGINNING OF WISDOM. . . ."*

....it follows the more a man fears the Lord, the wiser he is. Could this be so? When godly fear causes one to think about his future status in heaven, is that not a service? When it makes him careful about the investment of his life, is it not his friend? When he begins to fear the consequences of a wasted life, is not that a favor? Godly fear is the friend of fallen man, not his enemy.

The fear of God motivated the greatest heroes of faith. Consider Abraham, the giant of them all. Who hasn't thrilled to the story of his offering of Isaac on Mount Moriah? That aged and trembling hand was ready to plunge the knife into the lad when it was stayed. But the old man feared God so much he dared not disobey. How do we know? God Himself commented on his amazing demonstration of faith:

"Lay not thine hand upon the lad . . . for now I know thou FEAREST GOD, seeing thou hast not withheld thine only son from Me!" (Gen. 22:12).

FEAR moved Abraham to faith. God said so. That's God's voice recorded in that verse. God accepted the offering

*Psalm 111:10

of Isaac as proof Abraham feared the Lord. Then we have the word of the Apostle Peter to consider.

> **"And if you address as Father, the One Who impartially JUDGES each man's WORK, conduct yourselves IN FEAR during the time of your stay on earth"** (1 Peter 1:17).

"FEAR GOD!" says Peter, counseling us to spend our **entire lives** in the fear of God. Notice his reason — **the judgment!** Look what is judged. Not us, of course, but... **"each man's work."** The very thing this book heralds. Dear reader, here is a truth which ought to be shouted in the ear of every Christian.

Listen again to the Apostle Paul. He says it is fear of the Lord which moves us to holy living:

> **"Therefore, having these precious promises, dearly beloved, let us cleanse ourselves from all defilements of the flesh and spirit, perfecting holiness in the FEAR OF GOD!"** (2 Cor. 7:1).

● Because we are fallen and sinful (though saved through faith in Christ), fear is a **necessary force** for moving us to rightful action. How glorious it would be if love and gratitude could do it. But alas, our condition is such, those virtues are not nearly so effective. It is **not** our passion for safety awards which makes good drivers of us, is it? No, it is the FEAR of getting killed or arrested. Who'd bother with careful driving if there were nothing to fear? So — who'd bother with a careful investment of his life in Christ, if there were no consequences for disobedience and indifference?

PAUL FEARED GOD'S JUDGMENT

I have declared the apostle's warning:

> "For we must all appear before the Judgment Seat of Christ, that each may be recompensed for his deeds in the body, according to what he has done, whether GOOD or BAD" (2 Cor. 5:10).

We emphasized those words GOOD and BAD. The **recompense** for BAD equals the CONSEQUENCES mentioned in Chapter One. This is what is frightening. No one is going to get away with ignoring his stewardship in Christ. He is a servant, like it or not. He has to turn in a report of his job, whether he does it or not.

Consider a servant. His master gives him a task. It is up to that servant how well he performs it or whether he does it at all. Then he receives a summons. He is asked into the master's office. His report is called for. How will he feel if he has gone about his own affairs rather than carrying out his master's orders? This could easily be the most terrifying thing any servant must face.

This is how the Apostle Paul feels. After his warning, he continues. . . . . .

> **"Knowing therefore the TERROR of the Lord, we persuade men . . ."** (2 Cor. 5:11).

Paul speaks of the **consequences** of the judgment. When he considers the recompense for EVIL works, tinges of terror touch his heart. This judgment will meet the consequences of sin and waste in our lives. We all have jobs for Jesus. All are His servants. Paul says the coming judgment will ask for our accounts. We will be rated for the way we have discharged our responsibility. The judgment motivated him.

Why did the Apostle burn himself out across the face of Asia Minor? Was it because he loved to travel? No. Was it fun for him to suffer beatings, imprisonment, and shipwreck? Was it a passion for punishment which finally led him to execution? Indeed not. He was motivated. A secret **terror** lurked in his soul. He says so, we have his statement on it. He dreaded the idea of being unworthy before the Lord (Phil. 1:20). He worked hard so as not to be a "castaway" (1 Cor. 9:27). He tells us what the Lord wants. . . . .

> **"Moreover it is required in stewards, that a man be found faithful"** (1 Cor. 4:2).

That's what the Lord DEMANDS of all His servants — **faithfulness.**

● HEY! JUST ANOTHER MINUTE THERE!

I think I hear a protest.

> "I can't bring myself to serve the Lord out of fear. I still think we should serve Christ out of love for what He has done for us. Fear seems like a poor reason for serving anyone."

I have no objection. If love can motivate you as well as fear, that's fine. BUT. . . .it must **not** be human love. You know, that giddy emotionalism which whispers. . . ."I love you." That affectionate quality which says, "I like being with you." That kind of love won't do. If one is to serve the Lord on the **basis of love,** it will have to be GOD'S LOVE, not man's. God's love is different, you know. It is based on sacrifice and obedience. It is neither a matter of affection nor of admiration.

> **"He that has my commandments and keeps them, he it is that loves me"** (John 14:21).

If your love for Jesus **drives** you to obedience, you can ignore my exhortation. If your **one passion** is to fulfill the Master's command, and you are **doing so** to the exclusion of all else, I am thrilled with you. With that kind of love at work in you, you won't fear the judgment — you'll welcome it. If you are satisfied that love for the Lord is bringing you to obedience better than fear, I yield the point. The important thing is your unswerving **obedience**.

But if you are like myself, the sense of what I ought to be for Christ, doesn't do in me what it should. I don't come anywhere near serving Jesus with the obedience due a Master. It causes me to do some things, but it doesn't **grip** my soul as does the terror of the judgment. It doesn't **spur** me to submission as much as the thought of **accountability**. It doesn't **compel** me to commitment as fully as those eternal **consequences**. The day of my accounting is the most dreadful fact of my life. But it isn't right for me to assume all Christians are as sinful and self-willed as I.

Therefore I am not concerned whether it is love or fear at work in you ....as long as you are motivated. The point of this book is your **awareness** of the day of accounting. I want you ready. If **divine love** sets your heart aflame so that all that matters, 60 seconds out of a minute, is implicit obedience to Jesus, fine. If your love **drives** you to exalt Him everyplace, doing His will continually, great! If you are His **bondslave** in chains of love, praise the Lord. If love moves you to readiness for that day, Hallelujah!

But if it doesn't, be honest with yourself. JUDGMENT lies ahead. I want you ready, regardless of what it takes to motivate you. You will be giving an account of your stewardship. You will reap the consequences. The day approaches with every tick of the clock. We must ALL be ready.

A criminal who had been in court often, was scheduled to appear once more. When he heard the attorney who had defended him on previous occasions was to be the trial judge, he relaxed expecting to escape a serious sentence. But his feelings quickly changed when the judge leaned over the bench to speak to him:

> **"When I was your attorney, I defended you the best I could. But I am no longer an attorney. It is not my business to defend you now, but to judge you. And I shall judge you as earnestly as I defended you."**

● Christians who relax, thinking their friend Jesus will not judge them seriously, have a shock coming. They will find **"there is no respect of persons with God."** The reason they appear before this court is because they are His friends. His enemies appear before another bench — the Great White Throne. Is He still our friend? Yes. Lover of our souls? Yes. He's all that, but He is also JUST. His friendship with us will never be allowed to compromise His justice. He will not be mocked even by His friends. Any man who truly loves the Lord, would not want to mock Him with disobedience.

● As far as the Lord is concerned, He has entrusted each of us with time, ability and a job which fits us to a tee. He expects us to be faithful. He longs for us to show as much concern for His interest as He has shown for ours. The Apostle John has also warned about this. His counsel is no less fearful. Hear his caution to those who lightly view the abiding life and fail to bear the fruit they should:

> **". . . that when He shall appear, we may have confidence and not BE ASHAMED before Him at His coming"** (1 John 2:28).

The Greek makes that read. . . .**"to shrink from His presence in shame."** Those fearful words are for those who spurn their servitude, who shun His Lordship over their lives. Are they not His, still? Indeed. He bought them. But they do not fear Him, consequently they disregard His commandment. When Christians live as though they **were not** the property of the One Who bought them, they have every reason to be terrified at the approach of that day.

IT MOTIVATES ME

In fact it is downright shaky to read. . . . .

> **"Our God is a consuming fire!"** (Heb. 12:29).

Picture what that could mean to a servant whose life consists of nothing but tissue paper and tinder. That's what a Christian accumulates when he lives for himself. A puff of smoke is what the judgment promises him. And then he will be found with **nothing**. You've bought firecrackers. You know how it is. Bang — and then there's nothing.

One day we will stand before His Honor, the Holy Judge. We will feel the scorching heat of His impartial gaze, the penetrating sweep of His searching eyes. What if there is a flash and all He beholds is consumed. And then you are found naked, destitute and unworthy before Him — and the heavenly host! Doesn't that make you squirm? I'll be His slave first. I'll give up the privilege of being my own boss before I'd take a chance that a **good God** won't judge His servants.

Who is foolish enough to GAMBLE that GOD'S law of the harvest won't stand? That even if it does, He won't apply it to His own? Is it like God to apply His Law against some and exempt others? He would show "respect of persons" if He did. The Christian who ignores the truth of the Judgment Seat of Christ is GAMBLING that God's Word won't stand. That's the folly of remaining indifferent to slavery in Christ. To question the fact of judgment is to doubt the durability of God's Word:

> **"The grass withers, the flower fades, but the Word of God stands forever"** (Isa. 40:8).

By now you can sense even more of my feelings as I chatted with the friend so pleased to have me serve the Lord while he let "Jesus do it all" for him? I thought to plant a provoking idea in his mind, hoping it might continue to work after I had gone:

> "Would you think about this, my brother . . . ? What if you are wrong? Suppose it is true that you are called to be the servant of the Lord and one day you must account for your stewardship at the judgment? You will lose everything. Your whole future will be forfeited. But let's suppose I'm wrong and you're right. What will I lose? Nothing but the pleasures and pastimes of life on earth. I will still have the joy of heaven ahead of me. Sure, I may have forfeited some ease, but I haven't risked my future. What's more, I'm doing it for Someone Who has already invested Himself in me!"

THE JUDGMENT — BIBLICAL CURIO OR CRISIS?

Consider the challenge I put to my friend. Would a Las Vegas gambler accept such odds? Never in this world. That would be like selling your sun glasses for 25¢ because you doubt the sun will rise the next day. Or let's say you are in your rich uncle's will to inherit one million dollars. The old man is in the hospital, near death. Then someone offers you ten dollars cash for your inheritance. You are faced with the gamble that your uncle will never die. Would you consider such a thing? No one in his right mind would. Or would he?

The Bible tells of a man who did. His name was Esau. He sold his inheritance to his brother Jacob for a bowl of red lentil stew (pottage). And this was no doubt the richest family in Palestine. Esau's father was very old and sick in bed at the time. You wouldn't think people in their right senses would be so foolish as to discount the future for the present, but they do, all the time. Any Christian who gambles that he will not have to appear at the judgment to surrender an account of his service as a slave of Christ, is as foolish as Esau. Think how many are trading their eternal fortunes for peanuts of pleasure.

What they are gambling is this: that God's Word doesn't mean what it says and even if it does, God will somehow immunize them because they have Christ as their Saviour. They really think they can live for themselves, indifferent to the Master's orders and get away with it. Well, that's the challenge I left with my friend. And I know he is thinking about it.

A BIBLICAL FACT

The Word of God cites three separate judgments:

1. **The Judgment Seat of Christ**—Only God's children appear at this judgment (2 Cor. 5:10). They are judged (compensated) on the basis of their stewardship of this life. The results of that judgment are eternal, therefore the consequences are lived out eternally in heaven.

2. **The Judgment of the Nations**—occurring prior to the millennium and having to do with the Gentile nations. Those nations on earth at this time will be awarded their places and roles in the earthly kingdom on the basis of their treatment of the Jewish people (Matt. 25:31-46).

> **NOTE:** Should anyone ask what is so special about the nation of Israel, the answer is — **nothing.** God made promises to the first Jew, Abraham, and they pertained to his earthly descendants. The Jewish race is favored because God keeps His promises, not because of their merit. With nations still on earth at that time, it is interesting to find that mankind is not going to be abolished by atomic warfare.

3. **The Great White Throne Judgment**—Where all the unbelieving dead appear before God. They are awarded (sentenced) on the basis of their stewardship of this life (Rev. 20:11, 12). Apparently there are degrees of hell, with distinctions made between the good and bad works of non-believers. As Christians live out their judgment eternally in heaven, the unsaved live out their judgment eternally in hell!

In this book we are concerned only with the first judgment. Yet we examine all three to observe they have one thing in common: each is an EVALUATION of the **past**. The appraisal made determines the candidate's **future**. The point of ANY judgment is to weigh one's past performance to let it affect his future. Consider the man who robs a store. That past act is weighed by the judge or jury. Then his days in jail are determined. See — the past always determines the future — in any kind of judgment.

THE CHARACTER OF OUR JUDGMENT

There are six passages speaking directly to the character of Christian judgment. I shall make an exposition upon them to show the **eternal** LOSS we suffer when we fail to invest our lives in Christ. I feel the emphasis of these passages features the CONSEQUENCES of the judgment.

The first we have mentioned twice already. This time view it as a warning:

> **"For we must all appear before the Judgment Seat of Christ, that each may be RECOMPENSED (rewarded or penalized) for his deeds done in the body (earthly stewardship), according to what he has done, whether GOOD or BAD"** (2 Cor. 5:10).

Linger on two words, "recompensed" and "bad". That word "BAD" is a particularly strong term for EVIL in the Greek. What is easily overlooked, as people read this verse, is that it says we are RECOMPENSED FOR EVIL. Remember: we have already cleared the air on sin's guilt. This is not punishment for guilt. If you recall the boy and his bicycle, you'll remember that forgiveness did not bring back his bike. He suffered the LOSS of it, even though his dad forgave him.

What we find in the phrase, RECOMPENSED FOR EVIL, is not a matter of guilt, but the CONSEQUENCES of BAD WORKS. So now to another passage which opens the truth of LOSS at this judgment:

> **"for no man can lay a foundation other than that which has been laid, which is Christ Jesus.** (That is salvation. After that comes the life built on Christ.) **Now if any man build on the foundation with gold, silver, precious stones** (that's one kind of construction), **wood, hay, straw** (that's another kind), **each man's work** (his life investment) **will become evident; for the day will show it** (every act will be exposed), **because it is to be revealed** (qualified or measured against) **by fire; and the fire itself will test the quality of each man's work"** (1 Cor. 3:11-13).

Let's stop before proceeding to the next verses. We need a good look at these. They unfold the Apostle's insight to the judgment. Every reader should grasp the significance of Paul's words here. I'll list the observations. We'll try not to overlook anything.

OBSERVATIONS:

1. These are saved people at this judgment, **Christians.** The foundation for their lives is Christ. No one else has Jesus for a foundation.

2. Two kinds of lives can be built upon Christ; one of value and permanence —the other waste and futility. Can we be sure of the context? The Apostle measures these lives against FIRE. Fire in Scripture speaks of judgment. But more than that, in the passage we see that fire **determines the outcome.** See how one class of works (mineral) is refined by fire; whereas the other (combustible) is destroyed by fire.

3. The fire is applied only to the WORKS of a man and NOT to the man himself. The man is NOT judged by the fire, only **what he has built** on the foundation. In other words, what he has DONE with his life in Christ. Everything a man builds on the foundation is reviewed, his **total** life works.

4. See how the life works are REVEALED. It is a **revelation** meaning everything he has done or said **suffers exposure** (Luke 8:17). This day is not a private review, but a public exhibition. The tiniest details of servitude, the smallest investment one has made or withheld, will be seen by all. Also the sacrificial investment one makes of his time, talent and resources to carry out his task for Christ will be declared as well.

5. All that a person DOES during his life on earth is not only examined and exposed, it is also **tested and weighed.** That which survives the test (fire) is approved and remains as a good work for the Lord. That which goes up in smoke, is obviously a bad work. Some Christians are going to be shocked when they see how MUCH of their lives has been **wasted.** The more waste (bad works) the bigger the bonfire. Keep in mind we are speaking of the believer's WORKS, not the man himself.

Now we can move to the next two verses. They contain the most painful, piercing truth of this teaching:

> "If any man's work (life investment) which he has built upon it (the foundation-Christ) remains, he shall receive a reward. If any man's work is burned up, HE SHALL SUFFER LOSS: (that is usually read over very fast); but he himself shall be saved, yet so as through fire" (1 Cor. 3:14, 15).

OUCH!

Can you feel the fire? Even the imagination responds when we speak of being near fire. The sting of those verses is the word — LOSS. That is no slip of the lip. Paul meant to say that. Fire can bring loss, whether in this life or the next. The Greek word here for LOSS shows it to be ETERNAL. When God's judgment fire is laid against a Christian's works, only **what is left** brings a reward. The rest is gone — **forever!** There are no make-up classes in Christianity. There is no way to return to earth with the thought of "doing better next time."

This is the horrible truth of wasted lives in Christ. Those people who live for themselves will be sorry. They build lives of tinder and kindling, things which cannot abide the judgment fire. No one can earn a reward in heaven and simultaneously squander his opportunity in self-living. Neither can one establish a fortune in heaven by occupying with the things of this world.

FIRE!

You awaken in the night. The smell of smoke reaches your bedroom. A feeling of terror smothers your spirit. Flickering tongues of flame are reflected on the wall. Panic overtakes you. The kids! Then you hear the crackling sound. The house is fully on fire! You race to awaken the family. There's just time to grab clothing and rush into the night.

With everyone outside, you feel some relief. But what a sickening feeling to watch everything you own consumed before your eyes. Ever been around a family that was burned out like that? Then you know the feeling. They become charity cases in minutes. Fire has reduced more than one family from riches to rags — fast!

It's the fear of fire I'm talking about. It can motivate us.

Some Christians will be "burned out" at the judgment. Note those words, **"he shall suffer loss."** The Holy Spirit would have us picture someone who has just gone through a fire with only his life spared. That's what Paul means when he says, "...yet he himself shall be saved....**yet so as by fire!"** Some Christians will begin eternity completely wiped out by fire. They suffer the LOSS of everything because it was tinder.

A fire on earth is bad enough — but in heaven! And to stay that way forever, with no opportunity to recover — that should make all of us fear God's fire! Who wants to be a charity case in heaven? Some could be. Those who refuse Jesus' Lordship will live to regret it. But Christian servitude is not for sissies. It requires the forsaking of self, sometimes friends and family. But that is better than seeing your future go up in smoke. The Word of God warns that flames of judgment will consume every combustible part of our lives!

Remember our man who teases Jesus? We followed him to the gas station. He shunned to say a word for Christ, refusing even to get out of his car and leave a tract in the restroom. In fact, he wouldn't bother to drop a tract in a magazine he was holding. Well...that cost him. It is our own fault if we don't invest in Christ while we have the chance. Oh, those eternal consequences — the horror of Christian judgment!

● See now why I call FEAR Christian motivation? There is something to fear. God's Word says so. The Apostle knew this terror. Peter and John warn us. The New Testament urges us to go all out for Christ, doing as much as we can every day. Later in the book I'll give some specific steps for building GOOD works on the foundation. What I want you to sense now is the **danger of fire.**

We'll let God's ancient writer summarize this chapter for us:

> "Let us hear the conclusion of the whole matter: FEAR GOD and keep His commandments; for this is the WHOLE duty of man. For God shall bring **every work** into **judgment,** with every secret thing, whether it be **good,** or whether it be **evil"** (Ecc. 12:13-14).

See? This truth isn't new. Even the patriarchs comprehended FEAR — WORKS — JUDGMENT — CONSEQUENCES.

SHOCK TREATMENT

In this chapter we have collected passages which spell out the most awesome truth of Christianity. Summarized they look like this:

> Once a man receives Christ, the remainder of his life on earth is to be spent as a servant of the Lord. How faithfully he discharges his stewardship affects his eternal status. His works will be reviewed at the judgment to see how **faithfully** he has cared for his Master's interests. If he fails to take advantage of his opportunity, there is no way to recover from the loss after death. If he exploits the opportunity, he can enter heaven a wealthy man, to enjoy a position of authority in the eternal administration of Christ.

That is a frightening truth, particularly if you have been led to believe that just getting inside heaven is enough. It can stagger those who feel that once inside those "pearly gates" they have it made. The Christian who regards his life as his own to use as he pleases, has been deceived. The Lord Jesus expects His servants to place His interests above their own.

Those who do **will not be sorry;** He is a generous Person. Those who **do not** will bear the consequences. He is also a **just** Person. He has every right to ask His servants for an accounting:

"Ye are not your own. For ye are bought with a price, therefore glorify God in your body, and in your spirit, which are God's" (1 Cor. 6:19-20).

I believe this truth shines from God's Word like a diamond against a black velvet pad. Further, I believe the Holy Spirit urges every child of God to become submissive to that same Word. If what I have said can be established as the will of God, sincere Christians should resist the devil's wiles and take it to heart. Why not check for the Spirit's witness as I set forth the summary from God's Word.

BIBLICAL SUMMARY

1. The hour of judgment awaits us all:

> **"It is appointed for men to die once, and after this comes judgment"** (Heb. 9:27).

2. Every Christian must surrender an account of his stewardship.

> **"So then each one of us shall give an account of himself to God"** (Rom. 14:12).

3. Whether we like it or not, each of us is under obligation to consider himself a servant of the Lord:

> **"And He died for all, that they who live should no longer live for themselves, but for Him Who died and rose again on their behalf"** (2 Cor. 5:15).

4. We are deceived if we think we can somehow avoid the consequences of a wasted life:

> **"Do not be deceived, God is not mocked; for whatever a man sows, this he will also reap"** (Gal. 6:7).

5. There are two ways for a Christian to use his life. He can invest his time and substance in eternal things, or he can devote himself to the temporary things of this world. The judgment is like a torch. His works will either go up in smoke, leaving him destitute; or they will endure the fire unharmed, leaving him wealthy in heaven. The self-life produces only tissue and tinder.

"For no man can lay a foundation other than the one which is laid, which is Jesus Christ. Now if any man builds upon the foundation with gold, silver and precious stones, wood, hay, straw, each man's work will become evident; for the day will show it, because it is to be revealed with fire; and the fire will test the quality of each man's work. If any man's work which he has built remains, he shall receive a reward. If any man's work is burned up, he shall suffer loss; but he himself shall be saved, yet so as through fire" (1 Cor. 3:11-15).

6. Every Christian will be summoned to appear before God's "Judgment Seat" and the results of that judgment will remain either GAIN or LOSS for each individual:

"For we must all appear before the Judgment Seat of Christ, that each one may be recompensed for his deeds in the body, according to what he has done, whether good or bad" (2 Cor. 5:10).

7. The Apostle Peter teaches us that FEAR of this judgment should motivate and guide us throughout our earthly lives:

"And if you address as Father the One Who impartially judges according to each man's work, conduct yourselves in fear during the time of your stay on earth" (1 Peter 1:17).

8. The Apostle John, who speaks of the Lord's coming as the time of Judgment, warns Christians of the possible shame they could feel when He appears:

"And now little children, abide in Him, so that if He should appear, we may have confidence and not shrink away from Him in shame at His coming" (1 John 2:28).

9. We must take seriously the Lord's admonition to accumulate wealth in heaven. The frightful implication being, if we fail to do so, we will have none when we get there. No one else is going to earn it for us. Poverty in heaven appears a real possibility for those who refuse the Lordship of Jesus:

"Do not lay up for yourselves treasures on earth, where moth and rust destroy, and where thieves break in and steal; but lay up for yourselves treasures in heaven, where neither moth nor rust destroys, and where thieves do not break in or steal" (Matt. 6:19-20).

10. A man must decide WHERE he prefers to enjoy wealth, this life or the

next. It is impossible to set one's affections on worldly things and become rich toward God. A man must choose one or the other, he can't have both:

> **"No man can serve two masters; for either he will hate the one and love the other, or he will hold to the one and despise the other. You cannot serve God and Mammon"** (Matt. 6:24; Luke 16:13).

> **NOTE:** The underlying principle which makes the above statement true is found in the Lord Jesus' counsel: "For where your treasure is, there will your heart be also" (Matt. 6:21).

11. The Lord employed FOUR PARABLES to teach four distinct features or bases of our forthcoming judgment:*

a. The parable of the WISE steward, by which the Lord showed the foolishness of God's people in FAILING **to prepare** for the day of accounting **when they know** it is coming. The parable emphasizes the WISDOM of extracting all the spiritual wealth one can from this life in anticipation of the day when he will leave all else behind (Luke 16:1-13).

b. The parable of the talents. In this the Lord showed that while Christians have **DIFFERENT OPPORTUNITIES** in this life, it is a matter of how faithful each is in his **own** stewardship that counts. One's gifts and abilities have nothing to do with another's capacity to earn the SAME reward. A housewife who is faithful to her call, for example, can end up with as much treasure as Billy Graham or Charles E. Fuller. She is NOT competing against people occupying a different role in life (Matt. 25:14-30).

c. The parable of the mina (pounds). The Lord employs this parable to show how those with the **SAME OPPORTUNITY do compete** with each other. Those serving with **different degrees** of faithfulness, receive **different rewards.** This parable, and the one above, show that **faithfulness** will be rewarded by a responsible position in the kingdom (Luke 19:11-27).

d. The parable of the laborers in the vineyard. This parable teaches that TIME is **not** a controlling factor as God measures faithfulness.

---

*A full discussion of these four parables appears in the back of this book as an appendix. It is not inserted here so that the thought-flow may continue uninterrupted.

The Lord is not forced to consider longevity when evaluating a servant's real worth. Thus, time in service is neither a limitation nor an advantage. A late comer in Christ can earn as big a reward as someone raised to serve the Lord in a Christian home. Also, a noble servant struck down early in life can be equally rewarded with one who has spent years on the mission field. The willingness and intentions of the thief on the cross, for example, might qualify him for a job as Jesus measures men (Matt. 20:1-16).

12. It can be costly to follow Christ. For some it could mean pain and sacrifice. But the Lord views it as **earning** a reward. Therefore it is an **investment.** It is possible for a Christian to invest his total life in Christ to become extremely wealthy toward God. The rate mentioned by our Lord at which Christians can accumulate spiritual treasure, was 10,000%. Everything sacrificed for Jesus, whether fame, fortune or family, could be calculated on an exchange basis of 100 fold:

> **"And everyone who has left houses or brothers or sisters or father or mother or children or farms (the dear things of this life) for My Name's sake, shall receive a hundred fold, and shall inherit eternal life"** (Matt. 19:29).

> **NOTE:** The reference to 100 fold is simply an accommodation. It should not be taken literally, for it is probably more like a million fold and beyond that. It is an expression which means "many, many times." We should accept it as saying, **"No matter what it costs you to follow Jesus, you won't be sorry."** The Lord's compensation will exceed our fondest dreams (1 Cor. 2:9).

THERE NOW — THAT'S THE TRUTH

Unless I have mis-handled a mass of Scripture, it stands that Christ Jesus is not only our Saviour, He is also our Lord. It is one thing to TRUST Him for salvation, quite another to SERVE Him as Lord. Thus a Christian does **not fulfill** his responsibility by TRUSTING the Lord, he must also OBEY Him and reverence Him as Master. That Christian who refuses Christ as his MASTER will be sorry. And if he dies that way it will be too bad for him. You'll see why — next.

Chapter Three

READY TO DIE — AS YOU ARE?

READY?

Go to a funeral. Listen to the preacher carry on about heaven. He makes it sound so wonderful. He pictures the reunion of loved ones. He announces the end of all toil and the beginning of total rest. He paints a picture of solid comfort with people relaxing in glory, away from the struggle of life. He opens his Bible to prove it:

> **"And God shall wipe away all tears from their eyes; and there shall no longer be any death; there shall no longer be any mourning, or crying, or pain, for these first things will have passed away"** (Rev. 21:4).

Wow! Isn't that something! Everything man fears seems to vanish with that verse. Take away pain, sorrow and death. . . and what's left to terrorize? Nothing. Or at least that is what many Christians think. Some even feel the work of Christ is so complete it even makes their wasted lives blossom into fruitfulness. Others think God will equalize everybody, so that it doesn't matter how one lives on earth. Everything is going to be beautiful, they think. Has not our language taken the word "heavenly" to mean delightful and beautiful?

The Apostle Paul doesn't share this glorious view of death. If it ushers in the bliss so many expect, surely death must be the FINAL FRIEND of man. Yet Paul doesn't agree. He has an altogether different word for death. Right in the middle of his resurrection passage, he calls it. . . .

THE LAST ENEMY!*

*1 Corinthians 15:26

What does Paul see in death that he should give it such a name? What is so terrible about dying he considers it our last enemy?

● Death is the "last enemy" of the Christian, because it brings to an end his opportunity to **get ready** for heaven. Death closes the door on the last opportunity to extract anything **eternal** from this life. When death strikes our bodies we are through laying up treasure in heaven, we are through developing into the likeness of Christ.

Do you know a little about photography? I'm sure you know that pictures are taken with a camera. Inside is film. Who hasn't dropped off film at the drug store to have it developed? Then what happens? It goes through a process and then finished prints are returned to us. We're interested in that process as an illustration of: life — death — heaven.

It's not too complicated. There are three steps:

1. The developing stage is first. Your exposed film is placed in a developing solution. The image begins to appear. When the technician feels the image has reached its best, he yanks it out of the developer and momentarily places it in another solution.

2. This second solution is called the FIXER. It STOPS all development of the negative. The instant this fixing bath touches your film, all changes in the image stop — **instantly**. From that point on the negative remains the same, it never changes.

3. Then there's a final step. Your film is transformed into prints. That is, the image appears in **another form**. Your film has gone from the developmental to the **final** or DISPLAY stage. Then you receive a call saying your films are ready. Those finished prints show off the skill of the photographer as well as the technician who processed them.

Our Christian **growth — death — display** process is just like that.

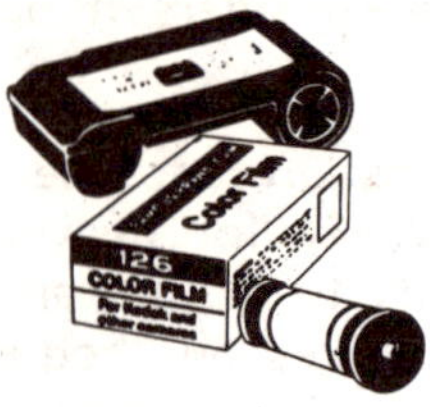

This life is a developing solution. Instead of chemicals, we are placed in **circumstances**. Our persons are the exposed film. The Master has put us in this world, the developing tank. When He feels the image has reached the best development He can hope for, He yanks it out of this life and places it briefly in the fixer. DEATH is the **fixer**. Once death touches the image of God, the development is arrested — **instantly**. From then on, there is **no more** development. The image stays as it is forever. Yet there is one more thing the Master does.

● He takes the developed negative (our person) and presents it in the new finished print (our eternal form) and displays it to its best advantage. There it stands as a testimony to our stewardship and to His work. Once those prints (ourselves in the new form) are on display, everyone will behold the genius and remarkable grace of God to reproduce His own image and bring it to His likeness. No two will be alike. That's to be expected when people are given the freedom of choice. But the variety will also stand as a testimony to His wisdom and workmanship forever!

God's Word speaks of the final stage:

> **"That in the AGES TO COME He might SHOW the exceeding riches of His grace in His kindness toward US through Christ Jesus"** (Eph. 2:7).

> **OBSERVE:** God makes **no changes** in the image once the developing process stops. There is no retouching of the negative, no remaking, no second takes. The work remains precisely as it comes from the developer. God doesn't make mistakes. You and I will enter glory exactly **as we are** when death strikes our bodies. We stay that way throughout all eternity.

We're the photographers.

We determine WHAT the image will be. God provides the conditions for bringing the image to the best possible portrait, but we supply the picture. He knows just when to remove it from the developer. He reserves that part for Himself. How do we take the picture? By polishing and perfecting our personalities as we meet the struggles of life. Every hurt, every abuse, every disappointment is calculated to shape us a little more like Him.

Every time we hold our tongues, return good for evil, speak kindly instead of critically, the image gets prettier. As the days go by, gentleness and graciousness should replace temper and sarcasm. As we show mercy to those who hurt us, understand those who abuse us, sympathize with the unruly, we become more like our God. As we sacrifice ourselves for others and patiently bear with our brethren when they are at fault, we take on more of the precious character of our Lord Jesus. But all this happens **only in the developer.** Finally, when God feels He has the best we are going to give Him, He yanks us out of the developer. When the image has become as Christ-like as He can hope for, into the FIXER it goes.

● Should death stop your development now, dear reader, you will enter heaven **as you are** right now. Your present patience factor is determined, your long-suffering quotient fixed, your gentleness stabilized, your meekness set, your goodness established — and that's it. As long as you are alive on earth, you can make changes. That's the nature of things in this life—**changing**. But once summoned to the judgment, it is all over. You will not be able to make one change into the likeness of Christ after that. That's the nature of things in eternity — **changeless**. Therefore this is the day of your opportunity.

IF I DON'T CHANGE, SO WHAT?

We enter heaven the very same people we are at death. Only a man's body dies. The person inside feels nothing. Neither does death change him in any way. Nothing happens to **you** when you die, other than release from your earthly prison. You won't even notice the transition from this life to the next — it happens too fast, "In the twinkling of an eye!" Bang — and there you are! You **feel** no different, you **are** no different.*

Someone has jokingly said:

> **"Man is like a tea bag, he doesn't come to full strength unless you put him in hot water."**

This is true. God puts man in hot water, a span of years on earth. The big opportunity, as far as our persons are concerned, is the ability to mature into the likeness of Christ.

Only on earth do we find the conditions for bringing people to maturity. Only on earth can the IMAGE of God be developed into the LIKENESS of God. The conditions necessary for CHANGING people are not found in heaven. But you know that. Many of you have read the details in some of my other books.**

It is on earth a man becomes a forgiving person. How does it come about? He has to be hurt by someone before he can forgive. Will there be any hurt in heaven? No. Then one cannot learn forgiveness there. How does

---

*See "Death: Graduation To Glory" where this truth is developed in detail.
**Faith Made Easy; Unequally Yoked Wives; Dynamic Truths For The Spirit-Filled Life

a man develop patience? By encountering anxieties and frustrations, learning to absorb them in stride. Are they found in heaven? No. And how does a man become long-suffering? He has to suffer a long time. But we read there is no suffering in heaven. Therefore, that trait too is developed on earth. So it is with every personality feature. Each is developed on earth where alone the conditions for **change** exist. There is no way for a man to **mature** in heaven, the **necessary stresses** are not found there.

See what this means? We have but this one life to CHANGE into the likeness of the Lord. Our personalities are formed as we REACT to His testings and trials of this life. What we finally become is up to us. We can be as sweet or sour as we like. We can let the blows of life shape us, or we can respond with hardness. We can remain the same person day in and day out, or we can let the circumstances of life change us every day.

What we become is **our** responsibility. We are the **stewards** of our own personalities. This is because we have free wills. God cannot make us free and then force us to be like Him. Neither can He create us like Himself. He is a good and generous Person because **He wants to be**. He would have us to be like Him because **we want to be**. Once you say I WANT to be, it becomes a matter of **choice**.

● God can only make us free. He can provide the conditions whereby we can mature in His likeness IF WE WANT TO, but He has no way of making us do it. Therefore, the development of our personalities is a genuine stewardship, one for which we must give an account. Right up until the moment death strikes, we can make CHANGES. But after that, we change no more. We will remain forever just as we appear before the Lord at the judgment.

Our works.

In earlier chapters we have seen that we are not only the SONS of God, but His SERVANTS, as well. Our sonship is a work of God. We receive it when we receive Christ. It is GIVEN to us, it comes from God. But Jesus is also our LORD. Service is what we GIVE HIM. Our servitude equals our submission to the LORDSHIP of Jesus. Again, see the difference in direction: God **gives us** sonship, we **give Him** obedience. It is like the two sides of a coin. Sonship is **from God** to us—service is **from us** to God. One does not eliminate the other.

● This book concentrates on our opportunity as **servants** of the Lord. It is our faithful service to an earthly task which qualifies us for our future job in heaven. At the end of our stewardship we stand before the Judge. He will measure our faithfulness by the yardstick of the parables. The reward we receive at that judgment is our future job for Jesus.

Both our PERSON and our WORKS are judged at death. Every day on earth is full of opportunities to serve the Lord and make changes in our personalities. Not one comes automatically. We extract them from each day. It is up to us how much we wish to squeeze from every twenty-four hours. Every day is an EMERGENCY in Christ!

Having said that, may we note again that our life on earth is one of CHANGE. Every second is vital to the life to come. One of the most sickening things for God to behold is a CHANGELESS CHRISTIAN. Every hour should be squeezed for what it can do to make us more like Jesus. Life on earth is designed to be one **continuous change**.

I had a dear friend in seminary. He was preparing himself for the mission field. I continually asked him to go on the streets with us to witness, to visit the hospitals and jails to win souls. He deferred, saying he would have plenty of time to win the lost when he got on the mission field. Never once did he consent to accompany me on a soul-winning outing. He kept repeating, **"I'll do it when I get on the mission field."**

He went to his station. I had a chat with him when he returned on furlough five years later. He had yet to win his first soul. His time on the field was occupied building a school. He didn't like it one bit when I recalled his boast before he left, how that he was going to do his soul-winning as a missionary. He got the point. If a man doesn't win souls at home, he won't win them **anyplace**. Geography doesn't change a person. Only his location changes. He is the same no matter where he goes — **even to heaven!**

Some feel that way about Jesus. They haven't sacrificed themselves for His Name, they haven't longed to make Him the Absolute Lord of their lives — but they expect to do so in heaven. They are like my missionary friend. They don't do it here, but they expect to there. Well — they'll find that the transition won't change them a bit. They'll have no more passion for our Lord there, than they do here. The probability is they will have less. The pain and pressure of this life will be gone. They won't need Him then. They do now.

Our capacity for Christ is being developed.

Consider marriage. It is the center of life as we know it. What is it all about? It is a laboratory. It teaches us how to live with ONE PERSON. The Bible joins one man with one woman for life. Why? We're going to be devoted to ONE PERSON in heaven. Don't you find it ingenious that a man and a woman should become ONE FLESH during their lifetime, in anticipation of becoming ONE SPIRIT with Christ throughout eternity? (1 Cor. 6:17).

Marriage is an environment of **stress.** Yes, there is romance and bliss, but it is only a tiny part. Mostly it is a matter of compromise and sacrifice. When you take two people of differing passions, likes, dislikes, backgrounds and put them under one roof for life . . . and say to them, **"Now you stay that way until death do do you part,"** it's like clamping the lid on a pressure cooker. You know what pressure does to tough meats. It does the same to tough souls. In such an environment a man and a woman are to live EXCLUSIVELY for each other. Is it easy?

God never said it would be. He doesn't intend that it should. Those pressures are intended to make a man like Christ — if he **wants to change**. Everything needed to bring forth the Master's lovely personality can be found in our homes. All the trials and testings, pressures and possibilities are neatly packaged under one roof, with every bit of it calculated to prepare us to live with Jesus.

● You know how nice it becomes when a husband and wife begin to think alike, desire the same things, become tender with each other, gladly sacrificing for the other partner. Their joy mounts, their delight soars. The passing years find them closer in spirit. If people sweetly change through sacrifice and self-denial, they are getting ready to live with Jesus. Self-denial is the climate of heaven. If a man can learn to **enjoy it here,** he will **revel** in it there.

> A Christian, willing to pay the price for personal maturity, will not be sorry when death comes. Not only will he be more like Jesus, he will like Jesus more.

After our Master had counseled His disciples on the graces He desired in His people, He summed it all by saying. . . .

> **"Be ye therefore perfect even as your Father which is in heaven is perfect"** (Matt. 5:48).

This is the divine intention. God wants heaven filled with people like Himself. We are getting ready to live with a GIVER and a SELF-SACRIFICER. This one life is our time of preparation. We must acquire these graces while we can. If we don't, it will seriously diminish our capacity for Christ and ability to enjoy heaven.

JOB SECURITY

Sure. Heaven offers job security. Once you have struggled, competed, invested yourself, and finally won a place by the Lord's side, it can **never** be taken away from you. In the U.S., top government jobs are up for grabs every four years. But in heaven you enjoy the privilege of serving an ETERNAL Administration. That's what makes the sacrifice worthwhile. The character of eternity, remember, is CHANGELESSNESS.

Familiar with teacher-tenure? In the teaching profession, after one has held a position for a number of years, he is granted "tenure". That means he cannot be put out of his job except under the most extraordinary circumstances. It is something of a reward. People work hard to earn this security. But the Lord Jesus offers something better. We are guaranteed JOB PERMANENCY. Having secured our jobs through faithful obedience to our Master, we are assigned PERMANENT RANKS in His government. What makes them so secure? **"And of His government there shall be no end!"**

THINK OF THAT: a permanent place by His side!

About three years ago a brother came to see me. He was terribly burdened to serve the Lord. He was getting up in years, beginning to regret he had done so little for Christ. He seemed to sense that death brought judgment. Now it bothered him. He came to talk to me about it. He was thinking he ought to do something with the time he had left.

> **"I've lived pretty much for myself all these years. Making a living and raising my family has taken most of my time. You know how it is, everybody hopes to accumulate a little in order that his last years on earth might be a little easier."**

Yes, I knew how it was. But that wasn't his problem. He apparently had no trouble taking his ease — anytime.

> **"Some years ago I was sick. I thought I was going to die. I sort of promised the Lord if He would heal me, I'd serve Him when I got well. Time goes by, as you know, and somehow I never got around to doing it. Do you think you might be able to use me here at PC?"**

That was easy. His talents fitted our ministry. I assured him we'd be glad to have him. We always need more hands. There are many little tasks in a literature ministry. It takes a lot of doing to get these helps out to God's people. He would be a welcome addition. I let him know it.

● Well, I didn't see him for another year. I assumed his great sincerity had moved him to action someplace else. But no. When he came the second time, he told me he still hadn't gone into action for the Lord. When I asked why, he replied.....

"I'm waiting on the Lord."

That sounded good, but — a whole year — wasted. That wasn't

good, especially when he felt the burden of the Lord to get going. He asked if we could still use him. I assured him we had a number of jobs just right for him. We knelt in prayer, as we had before. He poured out his dedication to God with tears. Then he left.

Another year went by. Here he was at my door again. True to his pattern, he was greatly burdened, but had done nothing. The Holy Spirit was definitely prompting him to get going. He felt it, it was the source of his burden. I suggested that he take a job with PC and then let the Holy Spirit seal it one way or the other. He shook his head. . . . .

"No, I think I'd better wait on the Lord. It's too easy to get out of His will, you know."

Out of His will! That was funny. But what's the use of saying anything. You can tell when people prefer to fool themselves. So once more the conversation ended with lofty words of prayer. He shook with emotion. Majestic tones came from his lips as he told God how dedicated he was. I never saw him again.

● News reached me that he had again become ill and the Lord had taken him home. Apparently the Master knew more time in the developer wouldn't yield any more. So the man died **waiting on the Lord**. Imagine something as precious as that truth really is, being used by Satan to defraud this Christian. All the years I knew him, he was convicted, certain the Lord wanted him busy. The problem, of course, was his **will**. He wasn't willing, he just **didn't want to**. And Satan knew it. So the suggestion, **"wait on the Lord"** found fertile ground in his unwilling spirit. It gave him a noble excuse. Behind his pious words of dedication, the devil had deceived him into . . . "waiting." He died waiting.

ISN'T THAT SAD?

The more so when you consider I had counseled him along the very lines you are reading. He met these same truths. He died aware of the consequences of a wasted life. He just didn't want to compete. He wasn't about to trouble himself. He wasn't interested in a job close to Jesus. You wouldn't think Christians would shrug off that privilege, but they do. Many really don't care whether they are near the Lord or not. Even in heaven, they prefer to "do their own thing."

Now this man was nice. He was pleasant, his manner polite. He was easy going and owned a gentle disposition. He would have made a great servant of the Lord. He delighted in the Word of God, even if he didn't care to obey it. He was **selfish** when it came to Jesus. He wasn't about to invest in anyone but **himself.** In some ways, he had made progress in the development of his PERSON. You could see it. But when it came to his WORKS, there was practically nothing to consider.

Will the justice of God appoint him a common laborer? Maybe. Heaven will have its "flunkies." Certainly there will be low-ranking, non-responsible positions for those despising God's service. Heaven must have toilers as definitely as an army needs **privates**. Will our man like his job, will he mind having it forever? He may be unhappy with himself, for forfeiting his crown, but he will accept his low rank and praise God for His wisdom. He may find it is the best spot in heaven for him. No doubt he'll get used to it in time. Oops, I mean eternity.

● Will he be a pauper? That's easy to answer. He didn't bother to lay up any treasure. He can't have much in his pockets. Will he be a charity case? Not quite. I remember a conversation in which he told me he left some tracts once. And at least one of them was responsible for bringing a soul to Christ. That ought to earn a few pennies in heaven. We know that the Lord is faithful to keep that which is "committed unto Him against that day" (2 Tim. 1:12).

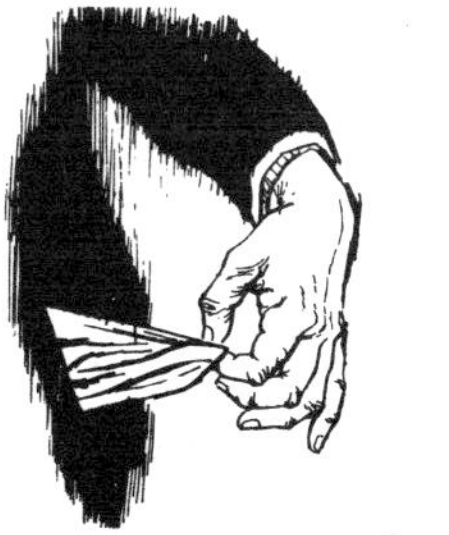

Flat broke in heaven! How does that sound to you? Some will be like that. Imagine, paupers in paradise! I don't want that. I've had my taste of poverty. I don't like it. I'll be a bondslave of Jesus before I'll risk poverty in paradise. I'll go without, suffer reproach, and work on my personality changes — whatever it takes. I want to be near my Lord forever. I want to be as close as I can get.

Who gets the high positions? Who will be the greats of eternity? The nobodies of this world. Those who have made no reputations for themselves, forsaking all to crown Jesus their absolute Master. Humble housewives who have submitted to harsh husbands as unto the Lord; faithful preachers who have loved God's sheep risking starvation before abandoning them; faithful witnesses who have proudly born the title "odd ball" and "fanatic", and those dear saints who sacrificed their jobs rather then be silent about the Savior — these scorned of the earth will be the giants of glory.

● I don't mind admitting I have my eyes on a job near Jesus. I can't say how well I am doing in His sight, but greed makes me covet a high position. He is faithful to see that what I do is not in vain. All I have to do is be faithful. One thing I do know, is how to acquire treasure. I've made one fortune in this life and parted with it. I am now working on my heavenly fortune by faith.

I have a friend who made a fortune selling food supplements. But he didn't do all the selling. He got others to sell it and he collected a tiny percentage on their sales. This is called an override. He had so many people out selling, he made a fortune off of the overrides. Some insurance people make big money this way too. Well, a lot of fortunes are made like that.

I secretly hope this book will send you into action for Christ. And when you start bearing fruit for Jesus, I'll get a wee cut. What could be more honest than that? It's fair. You accumulate your wealth as you get going. I merely get a percentage (not from you, but the Lord) from what you produce for the Master. The more people I can get into action for Christ, the bigger my override in the Spirit. So now my secret motives are in the open.

I think it important to say that, for the Holy Spirit uses frankness and honesty. He can bless it. Also, when Satan starts his hindering action, one of his suggestions could go like. . ."I wonder what Lovett expects to get out of this?" Then you'll know. I hope to accumulate spiritual treasure by getting more people into action for Christ. The more they make, the more I make.

I am anxious to challenge and equip every life I can with the know-how of Christian obedience. I don't want any of my brethren to end up in heaven flat broke. I know that shocks you. But it is possible, you see, for those who refuse the Lordship of Christ to reach heaven—penniless! Ugh! Can any Christian honestly believe that poverty in paradise will be any better than it is here! We'll see about that—next.

Here's the gist of what we've said so far:

WHERE WE WILL BE — **IS FREE**

Whether in heaven with Jesus or on earth with Him is matter of a free gift or an inheritance.

WHAT WE WILL DO — **IS EARNED**

Our future jobs with Christ, whether performed on earth or in heaven are being determined by our faithfulness now.

WHAT WE WILL BE LIKE — **IS DEVELOPED**

Our persons, i.e. our personalities are being developed in this life as we react to stresses and strains, testing and trials of every day life. Every day should find us more like Christ.

Keep those three concepts in mind and you will rightly divide the truths of judgment and our future with Jesus.

Chapter Four

THE GHETTOS OF HEAVEN

Once when I was struggling to get started on my own, I had to live on two meals a day. I ate but one meal on Sundays. That allowed me to save 10c a week. My Scotch grandmother taught me to set aside something, no matter how little I earned. Times were tough then. Our country was in the depression of the 30s. I hated being poor. I had a good taste of it and I don't like it. I know for sure, I don't want to be poor in heaven.

I DREAD BEING POOR FOREVER

Before I was saved, I lived to make money. I wanted to be a millionaire. Money was my God.

One day, when I was twenty-one years old, the phone rang. I answered. The voice said, **"This is your father speaking."** I heard my dad's voice for the first time. I was a wee baby when my parents were divorced. That was the beginning of excitement. Not only did I have the thrill of meeting my father for the first time, but he was in the building business and very successful.

It was natural that he should teach his son the ropes. I learned fast. Even got a little fortune started. Then came World War II. I took time out to serve Uncle Sam as a flying officer, even so I remained infected with dollar fever. I greedily saved all I could from my military pay. When I was released from active duty, I returned to constructing hotels and motels, selling them as fast as they could be built.

In something like eighteen months my personal fortune reached $868,000.00. I was approaching the million I wanted so badly. But then came Jesus. I was saved, quite by "accident" as some of you know from reading the book **Dealing with the Devil!** Shortly I was aware of the Lord's call on my life. But as God would have it, I was involved in a large corporation. My assets were part of the pool. I couldn't pull out without sacrificing a fortune.

It was a showdown. Would I yield the fortune and serve Jesus? Or would I cling to the money and remain a slave of mammon? The presence and power of the Holy Spirit made it possible to cast away the fortune. A thrill went with it. Even so, it was not easy for a greedy fellow like myself. God, however, used it to shift my obsession from money to Christ. Having passed through the money barrier, I was ready for the long trek through Bible college, seminary and graduate work in a state university. Ten years in all. It is amazing what the Holy Spirit can prod a man to do.

BUT I AM STILL GREEDY.

Coming to Christ didn't end my passion for wealth. I am still greedy, perhaps more so. But the **direction** has changed. I still want to be a millionaire — **but in heaven**. The idea of eternal wealth intrigues me even more than earthly wealth. Besides, doesn't a man have to leave his "mammon" behind when he dies? Eternal wealth, therefore, is far more inviting.

Do I feel bad about my greed in Christ?

No. I appreciate the Lord's genius to exploit a man's ambitions. He is so wise in motivating me. He knew exactly what it took to transfer my longings from earth to heaven. When He counsels, **"Lay up treasure for yourselves in heaven,"** He is talking down my alley. When He says, **"Where your treasure is, there will your heart be also,"** that is a perfect description of my nature. My heart does follow my treasure. Consequently the more I lay up in Christ, the more my heart becomes fixed on Him.

JESUS IS SERIOUS ABOUT HIS OFFER

At times, after I had committed my fortune to Christ, Satan would stab me with attacks of regret. Then the Holy Spirit would assure me that nothing sacrificed for Jesus is ever lost. His Word reminded me it was all laid up and waiting. What a wonderful Master. He not only makes me feel good about surrendering a fortune, He challenges me to invest more. The day the Spirit showed me I could earn 10,000% interest in Christ, my greedy soul shouted "Hallelujah!" From then on, I knew there was only one place to fix my ambitions—in Christ Jesus.

● Now if the idea of wealth in heaven is new to you, consider again the Lord's statement:

> **"Lay up for yourselves treasure in heaven"** (Matt. 6:20).

"For yourselves!" Did you get that? Turn that coin over and it says, **"If you don't lay up treasure for yourself, you won't have any when you get there!"** If this Word of our Lord is to receive credence at all, it means a man must EARN HIS OWN wealth for heaven or **have none** in eternity. Nowhere in the Word does it teach someone else is going to lay up treasure for us. It is fully our own responsibility.

A man facing a wall protested it was too high for him to climb. Whereupon his friend seized his wallet and tossed it over the top. At once the man scrambled over the wall to retrieve his money. Treasure made the difference. The story books are filled with daring tales of men who risked their lives for wealth. The magnetism of money appeals to the human heart. We have all heard of the desperate things people will do for a fortune.

We see the wisdom of the Master. He knows about this passion, and uses it. He knows if we get serious about treasure in heaven, it isn't long before we have too much laid up for our hearts to be any other place. Who can afford to be distracted when all of his wealth is concentrated in Jesus? The Apostle urges us to become serious about it:

> **"Since you have risen with Christ, shift your ambitions to heaven. Inasmuch as your Master reigns there, that is the place to invest. Purpose to be rich in the next life and discount, yea, even ignore the attractions of this one"** (Col. 3:1, 2 PNT).

The Lord knows the luring power of treasure. That's why He invites all of us to accumulate fortunes **by faith**. It is good business both for Him and for us. It makes sense.

But greed, can it be godly?

Yes, if directed heavenward. That's what makes it godly. It operates by faith. Faith changes the quality of greed. It becomes **spiritual** greed. The difference, you see, is **direction**. Godly greed, operating by faith is turned **heavenward**. Carnal greed is toward the **world**. See how it works? A man laying up treasure in heaven, deposits his wealth in a bank he **cannot see**. That makes it by faith. He earns it serving an **invisible** Lord. Again, by faith. He does all this on the Word of His Savior. He believes Him when He says, "You won't be sorry." This honors the Lord. It requires one trust His promises and forsake the promises of the world.

Have you thought how direction makes such a difference?

Consider another emotion — hate. It can be good. Develop a hatred for sin and God is pleased. God hates sin. When He sees this same hatred burning in His children, He is thrilled. Turn that same hate toward another Christian and it becomes evil. **The difference is direction**. Hatred toward sin is good, hatred toward others is evil.

A hunger, then, for God's reward is good. It honors Him. One must turn his back on the god "mammon" in order to **covet** God's gold. Our father is pleased when our **ambitions** are centered in Him. The more we deposit in heaven, the more confidence we show in His promises. Our greed for heavenly treasure is an accurate measurement of our faith in the Word of God.

An Evangelical church was holding a mountain retreat. The conference grounds were located in a hidden valley. It was necessary to mark the route for the first timers. At a fork in the road the highway divided. One road led over the hills into the desert, the other to the hidden valley. Some prankster turned the sign.

One little act, one wrong suggestion changed the day for many families. It was such a simple thing, just a **difference in direction**. An arrow was turned. Yet it took sincere people to the wrong destination. What was a second's work for a young imp, took a day out of the lives of many dedicated people.

● So it is with Satan. If he can reverse the arrow so that God's blessings are mistaken for heavenly treasure, he can mis-direct Christian lives. Christians make it easy for him. They help him. You know human nature. Isn't it nice to think that our rich God would give us all we could hold, simply because He had it to share? Don't some feel their rich relatives have an obligation to share their wealth with them? People are like that. Satan's suggestions fall on **interested ears.** Our Heavenly Father is rich, no question about that. But is He obligated to put His family on the dole? He won't. It is always better when people make their own way—even God's people!

Heaven's poor.

Imagine being poor in heaven. Terrible thought, isn't it? There could be multitudes like that. I assure you many are not interested in the Lord's invitation. There are Christians who don't think He means for us to invest in Him. But they will be sorry. Poverty will be no better there than it is here. Yet no one will ever be able to say the Master didn't make it clear. He certainly pressed the point often enough:

> **"Labor for that which endures unto eternal life"** (John 6:27).

. . . or again:

> **"Seek ye first the kingdom of God . . ."** (Matt. 6:33).

He is serious about it. He means to reward His servants for sacrifices in His Name. He not only calls us to another life, but invites us to compete for a place in it. Salvation is only part of heaven's appeal. God means for us to work to get ahead in the next life as surely as men compete to get ahead in this one. Notice again the double character of His promise:

> **"And they shall receive an hundred fold AND (plus) inherit everlasting life"** (Matt. 19:29).

See? Eternal life AND the 100 fold investing are two separate matters. Of course it is wonderful to be saved from hell, to be rescued from the fate awaiting those outside of Christ. Salvation is not to be minimized. But it is only the **beginning point** of a whole new life. Salvation is a birth process. It **starts** another life. That doesn't relieve a man from the responsibilities of that life. Does a birth into any life automatically guarantee one a future position in that life? An individual must always make his own way — here in this life or the next. Getting a man into heaven is God's part. What the man does with that privilege is up to him. With the Lord's interest rate so high, not one Christian should end up a pauper in paradise.

The Ghettos of heaven

The "ghettos of heaven!" Doesn't that bring a shock! Sadly, a host of God's people will be poor forever. Why? The justice of God will not be compromised. Satan deceives Christians into thinking God will somehow equalize the difference between those who obey Him and those who don't. And by some miraculous means, reward their wasted lives along with the faithful. The devil is clever about it. It is no small trick getting otherwise sober believers to think that those who squander life's opportunity will fare as well as those who go "all out" in living for Jesus. Listen to this wile:

> "Sure a person has to work to get ahead in this life. One needs to be industrious and conscientious. But in heaven it is different. Jesus does it all for you. He is so rich, you will have all you want because you are God's child. So forget about investing in Christ. It isn't necessary. There's wealth in abundance in heaven. More than enough for all who reach there. God is generous. He will see that His own have everything they want. Isn't that what heaven means?"

It sounds Christ-honoring. That's what's tricky about it. Christians enjoy that sound. They want to believe it. If Satan can keep them thinking that until they die, he can fill heaven with paupers. He knows human weakness. His suggestions always appeal to our lower natures. We want to believe God is so rich He will **give** us treasure in heaven.

DOESN'T HEAVENLY CITIZENSHIP MEAN WEALTH?

This very moment we are citizens of the kingdom. And because "our citizenship is in heaven," it is natural to suppose we are automatically entitled to the wealth of the land. But is it ever that way? Certainly it isn't true in the United States, an extremely wealthy country.

Citizenship in the U.S. is a wonderful thing. There is an amazing package of rights which comes with it. Many would pay a big price for this citizenship, if it could be bought. But it is not for sale. It comes as a GIFT to those born here, or qualifying under the law. But that doesn't mean our land has no poor. Citizenship doesn't **automatically** make Americans rich. We may be the wealthiest of all nations, yet we have slums and ghettos. America has her paupers. A wealthy country doesn't mean each inhabitant is rich.

Many are BORN citizens of heaven, but does that make them rich? Is the wealth of heaven **automatically** transferred to every child of God? Does every Christian have a mansion waiting, and a fat bank account? I'm afraid not. A man must work as hard to get ahead in heaven, as he does here. We could almost say that was the point of the parable of the unjust steward (Luke 16). Those who don't care about serving Jesus will have a place in heaven all right. But you and I don't want to live there. Who can honestly say he prefers a ghetto to a palace, the slums to the mansions? His sanity is in question if he does.

Citizenship in heaven is akin to citizenship in the United States. A precious package of rights goes with each. We discussed the salvation package in Chapter One, listing seven specifics. Each was something WE COULD NOT DO FOR OURSELVES. Those rights were not earned, but **bestowed** on each of us. The rights of an American are bestowed on him at birth. Every Christian has **every spiritual blessing** CONFERRED on him at the moment he is "born-again." And did we not find that these blessings **come down** from God, whereas our treasure is **laid up? That difference in direction should be kept in mind — always**.

BUT WHAT ABOUT OUR INHERITANCE IN CHRIST?

Here we go again. That word "inheritance," seems to suggest treasure, doesn't it? We automatically associate an inheritance with wealth. So when the word speaks of an inheritance in Christ, we assume it has to do with a fortune. We are used to having people die, leaving estates to heirs. But we do NOT inherit any kind of treasure, fortune or job in Christ. The sons of God are not made wealthy by a will.

But you say, "What about the verse describing us as heirs?'

> **"And if children, then heirs; heirs of God, and joint-heirs with Christ; if so be that we suffer with Him, that we may also be glorified together"** (Rom. 8:17).

That verse is famous. It sounds as if we jointly inherit some vast fortune with the Lord. There is no doubt that "joint-heirs" means sharing some kind of an inheritance. But what does the **Lord** inherit? When we answer that, we'll know exactly what it is in which we share. Hang on to the word..... "SHARE."

But first: even though our Savior walked the earth in a body, appearing as an ordinary man, He was no less than the great I AM and said so (John 8:58). Though men were allowed to put Him on a cross, He was no less than the Eternal God in human form. True, He divested Himself of outward majesty for the time of His humiliation, but He DID NOT divest Himself of His Divine Being. He would then have ceased to exist. He appeared as a Carpenter, but He was still the Deity. During all of His earthly sojourn, He was GOD.

Consequently — when He died, **He did not** INHERIT HEAVEN. That was ALREADY HIS as the Sovereign of Glory. When He died — better, when His body died — He **resumed** what He laid aside to step into the human stream. He took again what He had left behind. He did not inherit the Glory of Heaven. It was always His.

What then is His inheritance? What is it that we are to share with Him?

The inheritance of the Lord is EARTHLY. If it is something He **inherits,** it has to be earthly. Why? He inherits it from His **Father.** For that to occur, He must be in the role of a SON. It is as the SON that He inherits from His Father. And Jesus' role as SON has to do with the earth, not heaven. There is something He inherits on earth. What? The privilege of returning in POWER and GLORY. The Carpenter comes back! But not as a Carpenter. . . .**as a KING!**

The Lord Jesus will appear a second time, but not in humility. He will arrive in the clouds as the GLORIFIED SON of God. The earth will behold the same Jesus coming. . .**"in the glory of HIS FATHER with the holy angels"** (Mark 8:38). But don't miss the fact that He is STILL in the **role of the Son.** Having fulfilled all that was required of Him, by His cross, He returns to be HONORED on earth as He is in heaven. And He invites us to be His joint-heirs, to share it with Him:

> **"Come ye blessed of MY FATHER and inherit the kingdom of God prepared for YOU!"** (Matt. 25:34).

There! that is our inheritance! It is prepared for us. The "come ye" is our Master's invitation to SHARE in His earthly inheritance as "joint-heirs" with Him. **It takes place on earth.** Our joint-inheritance with Christ has NOTHING to do with our eternal sonship in heaven. It has to do only with the privilege of APPEARING WITH HIM on earth to taste the glory which accompanies His EXALTATION. Today we feel the bitter barbs which are yet a part of His humiliation. But one day we shall see our dear Master high and lifted up before all peoples of the world.

How do we share in it?

When the Lord Jesus reigns on His earthly throne, what will we do? Merely sit and soak, basking in His admiration? Hardly, we'll be busy. Doing what? Almost precisely what we'll be doing in heaven, certainly the counterpart of it. By that I mean the physical expression of whatever our jobs are in the spirit. **We'll have the same jobs.** Those jobs will correspond to our jobs in heaven. How can we be sure? That's why we pray "Thy Kingdom come." The kingdom on earth is an EXTENSION of God's will, i.e., an extension of heaven. His will is to be done on earth. . .exactly as it **is in heaven.**

Therefore, it is almost certain we will enjoy the SAME RANK on earth, that we hold in heaven. The task we perform on earth, **though occupying physical bodies,** will be akin to the one we perform in heaven. Without doubt this has to do with the exercise of some kind of authority.

● Rank, as you recall is EARNED. The job we do for Jesus, whether in heaven (in the spirit) or on earth (in the kingdom) will be the one for which we have QUALIFIED ourselves. Should it make any difference **where we are?** If the will of God is being carried out, does it matter whether we are on earth or in heaven? We should not, therefore, confuse our EARTHLY INHERITANCE, which is merely the PRIVILEGE of **being with Christ on earth** with our RANK or JOB, which is earned. Being with Him in the earthly kingdom is INHERITED, what we do with Him there, IS EARNED.

> **NOTE:** Being with the Lord in heaven is a GIFT. Being with the Lord on earth an INHERITANCE. Therefore no matter WHERE we are, the privilege of being there is either a gift or an inheritance. We do nothing to make ourselves eligible to BE WITH the Lord any place. On one occasion He prayed . . . "Father, I pray that those whom Thou hast given Me, BE WITH ME, to behold My glory . . ." (John 17:24). The matter of WHERE we are, is God's answer to Jesus' prayer request. And . . . **"so shall we ever be with the Lord"** (1 Thess. 4:17). The great verses closing the eighth chapter of Romans teach that nothing can separate us from Jesus. So whenever He changes location, we do too.

Does that help?

I don't mean to go on and on with biblical technicalities. It is quite simple, but Satan veils the truth. Maybe I can restate it in still simpler terms:

- The Lord Jesus forfeited His glory in heaven.
- In obedience He came to earth to redeem us.
- He will be rewarded on **earth** for His obedience.
- We forfeit the glory of this life to live for Christ.
- In obedience we live for our unseen Lord.
- We will be rewarded **in heaven.**

There is a bonus feature. The Lord Jesus has invited us to share in **His reward,** His earthly kingdom. Call it a PLUS, if you like. He wants us on earth with Him to see His glory. **The privilege of being there is our inheritance**. Satan would trick us into thinking the privilege of being with Christ (our inheritance) automatically makes us rich.

Satan's logic is simple. If he can confound the idea of our inheritance with the necessity for laying up treasure, he cancels Christians. Who bothers working for a treasure he expects to inherit? If he can make men think their status as "joint-heirs with Christ" assures them of gold in glory, why should they compete for wealth in Christ?

WHAT WILL WE DO IN HEAVEN?

Heaven is a big place, a busy place. Of necessity there will be some system of command. All kingdoms require a descending order of powers (administrators) to operate smoothly. Even Satan's kingdom has a hierarchy of powers (Eph. 6:12). The top jobs, naturally, carry the most authority. They will be the **closest to the throne,** just as the cabinet officers are closest to the president in our country. Authority is exercised over PEOPLE. People are the treasure of heaven. We need not press the point beyond the idea of authority over people, otherwise we could trespass matters beyond the scope of the Word of God. That's foolish.

We can use military language to speak of heaven. An orderly descent of powers indicates a CHAIN OF COMMAND. Whether in business or politics, it takes graduations of authority to make masses of people function as a unit. There will be **order** in heaven. That is inescapable. To have order, there must be ranks and rows, there must be those who give orders and those who receive them. When Jesus fed the five thousand, He had the men sit in orderly rows for fair and expeditious distribution of the bread (Mark 6:39, 40). That miracle required ranks and administrative order. Heaven will not require less.

This means there will be a descending order of positions from the Lord Himself down to the lowest servant in heaven. The ranks will descend from the Commander-in-Chief to the least private. The higher the rank, the **closer** one will be to Christ. If a Christian longs to be near Jesus throughout eternity, it should drive him to faithful service in this life. Above we spoke of treasure in heaven. Now we can define it more precisely. What we are really doing is qualifying for a place close to Jesus. When we speak of a good job with Jesus, we mean more than high position in His administration. We are thinking of proximity. Some Christians will be closer to Christ than others. They've earned a place by His side. You can be sure that eternal nearness to the Lord will be the award for faithfulness in this life.

● Shouldn't you covet a place by His side? This is what I mean by godly greed, the longing to be near Him — **forever!** You are as eligible to compete for a high place in the palace as anyone else. And when you have won it, you will remain close to Christ eternally. So now when I speak of treasure in heaven and of jobs with Jesus, you know what I really mean. The Bible uses such language because good jobs and money in the bank are terms we understand. That's why I use them too. Yet, in spite of these language symbols what we're really talking about is a permanent place at the side of the Saviour. If you were to die right now, how close to Christ do you think you'd be? That's why this book talks about **getting ready** to die. Sure—a person can get ready. The next chapter gets you started.

Chapter Five

ENTERING THE ARENA

A newly married couple bought an unfurnished house. Before moving in, they departed on a honeymoon tour of Europe and Asia. Traveling from country to country, they ran across many wonderful objects. They found numerous items which would be nice in their new home. Every time they discovered something particularly fine, they would buy it and ship it back to the United States. The objects ranged from knickknacks to lovely furniture pieces.

When they returned to America it was all waiting for them. They were able to dress their home in great style. Not only was it a show place, but it was theirs for a fraction of the cost in U.S. dollars. They began to live amidst a treasury of memory. Each object helped to recall the delight of their honeymoon.

WE CAN DO THE SAME

I won't say that slavery in Christ is a honeymoon, but it leads to one. You've heard of the "Marriage of the Lamb," and how we are called the "Bride of Christ." We are headed for a honeymoon. Before this chapter ends you will think of yourself on a trip with the same possibilities as that honeymoon couple. It's possible to extract good things from this life and send them on ahead. Do we not sing. . . .

> **"This world is not my home, I'm just a passing through,**
> **My treasures are laid up, somewhere beyond the blue:**
> **The angels beckon me from heaven's open door,**
> **And I can't feel at home in this world any more."**

We are "pilgrims and strangers" passing through this world. We can select the precious things from this life and send them on to our home in heaven. When we do, we are "laying up treasure."

Close to where I live a supermarket held a contest. The prize was the privilege of going through the store and leaving with all you could collect and carry in five minutes. I was there when the prize winners poised for the starting gun. Bang! They were off!

You should have seen the fury with which those people shoved and grabbed at the shelves. In desperation they pushed and piled their carts as high as they could. Some cried because they couldn't move faster. Everything in the store was available to them. There was no limitation except TIME. We spectators roared with laughter, but those contestants were deadly serious.

It's like that with us. The world is our supermarket. The only limitation is 24 hours. We can't stretch that. But within that span, everything we do and say for Jesus adds treasure to our account. Everything we sacrifice or suffer for Him, is like spiritual gold. Shouldn't we be more eager than those grocery grabbers? They scrambled for perishable food. We race to win an imperishable crown, and everlasting jobs.

Every day is loaded with opportunities to serve Christ. If one doesn't hit you in the face, you can create one. It might mean a tract left in the restroom, or a word to the waitress before you leave a restaurant. Or it might be when you prevent an unpleasent situation at church or kneeling with a derelict in a midnight mission. Then again it could be rescuing a man out of gas or taking kids to Sunday school in your car. What matters most is doing it because you are an eager servant of the Lord. Once you accept Christ's lordship as a way of life, the invitation to compete for points is wide open:

> **"Whatsoever you do in WORD or DEED, do all in the Name of the Lord Jesus . . ." (Col. 3:17).**

That word....''Whatsoever''...makes the invitation unlimited. You and I can do **all we want to** for Jesus. There is no limit to what a man can accumulate in a day. A greedy Christian can view the 24 hours of a day as good for just one thing — piling up points in Christ. Put that way, slavery in Christ sounds more like adventure than drudgery. In many ways it is very exciting.

Against the clock.

Military installations use the 24 hour clock. Ever see one? The small hand goes around once in 24 hours. A Christian has 24 hours. They belong to his master. Normally he sleeps eight of those hours, yet that doesn't make them his. That leaves sixteen. Of the 16, eight more are used for an employer. . . .that leaves eight. What of them? Generally they are taken up with dinner, relaxing, shopping, enjoying recreation (TV) or fun with friends. Then comes the weekend. The schedule is altered some. Those eight hours, normally devoted to an employer, become his to do with as he pleases. Oh, oh, pleases?

American living romanticizes **leisure**. We're going to hear more of this word in the future. Business forecasters predict a boom for those dealing in leisure products, i.e., campers, sporting goods, mountain homes, etc. The word leisure, though, should make a conscientious Christian cringe. If TIME is his most valuable possession, leisure is not only profane — it is prohibited. For those getting treasure from this life while the getting is good, "leisure" is stricken from the vocabulary.

When it comes to competition in Christ, it doesn't matter whether we are speaking of a work week or the weekend. The TOTAL TIME of a servant belongs to his master. The only "time out" is for spiritual refreshment. That is proper. And better when enjoyed systematically. That way a person doesn't over-indulge. What is refreshment for a serious servant? Church provides a nice "time out" for those prospecting for points in the world. It is in order to think of church-going as "time out" from the competition in Christ.

CHURCH . . . Christian refreshment

The habit calls for weekly gatherings in special buildings. This can be refreshing. Christian fellowship is wonderful recreation, a **necessary** recreation. Besides, a few servants can earn EXTRA points by teaching or preaching. That can be invigorating after steadfastly serving Christ all week. I know,

I'm a pastor. I relax from my labors for the Lord by preaching to my congregation. It refreshes me. It prepares me for another week's work for Christ in the world.

Of course, no man serious about a job with Jesus would think of substituting a church service for his own personal service. Anyone knows that sitting in the stands at a baseball game is not the same as being down there on the diamond. Those relaxing in the pews are "taking in." That is not the same as "putting out," which you must do in competition. Enjoying an event as a spectator is not the same as participating as a contestant.

I probably didn't need to say that. But Satan might have some reader buffaloed into thinking that going to church was the same as serving Christ. Except for those very few who earn **extra points** by ministering to the brethren, church going is better thought of as "time out" for Christian recreation.

Consequently, I have no criticism of the CHURCH as she operates within evangelical Christianity. She is doing well in view of the late hour of history. If I were to make any recommendation, it would be to suggest that members be taught the art of satanic warfare. It would seem a shepherd should secure his sheep from the wolf as well as fatten them in the Word. Without some defense against the devil, they become richer and juicier prey. I wouldn't mention this, were it not my call to supply the KNOW-HOW.

You can see how convenient it is for Christians to blame an INSTITUTION (the church) for their personal failures. She makes a nice target. And Satan is eager to sponsor any attack against the body of Christ. One of his devices is to suggest that organized bodies of Christians are somehow the spiritual machinery for world-evangelism. It simply isn't true. Christianity is a fellowship. We have been invited to fellowship with the Father and the Son (1 John 1:3). The outward social form of Christianity is a fellowship of believers. And that's all. It is not an institution, neither is it some kind of big business. However, I don't think it is improper to regard the church as a barracks for the soldiers of Jesus Christ (2 Tim. 2:3). Where else can the average Christian be trained in the skills of sharing Christ with others?

THE ARENA

Without argument the arena of Christian competition is **not in the church**. It is the world. The Commission says so, specifically:

"Go ye into all the WORLD".

Going into the world and working in a church are hardly the same. The church and the world are opposites. They are even headed in different directions — one toward God, the other toward Satan. It requires some fancy twisting of the Word to make the **church** and **world** the same. Why would anyone want to do so? Only to show, perhaps, that going to church was somehow a fulfillment of the Great Commission. And why would a person want to do that? Surely his motive would be suspect.

The "YE" of the commission is **personal**. Individuals are sent. But where? Can a man reach the entire world by himself? That's ridiculous. The world into which each man is sent, is his own ....PRIVATE WORLD. Only individuals can reach their private worlds. Within your private world are people you can reach better than anyone else. Around you are souls you can influence for Christ better than Billy Graham. In fact, there are people you can touch and penetrate for Jesus better than anyone else in the world. The Lord calls you to do that when He says.....

"Ye shall be My witnesses . . ." (Acts 1:8)

YOUR PRIVATE WORLD

GETTING STARTED

It has taken us a little while to get here. We've covered a lot of ground so far. Entering the competition is serious business. I am hoping you have reached the place where you feel it is the only thing to do. You will laugh when I make the next point. I am going to give you an assignment. It's tongue in cheek, of course.

Assignment: wait until dark. No one is to see you do this. Go out of the house. Look up and down the street. The coast is clear. Do you see any cars parked at the curb? There's one a few doors away? Good. Now walk boldly to that car and witness to it. Slap it on the fender, look it squarely in the headlight and tell it, it needs to be born again.

Could you do that? Sure. Cars offer no threat. They can't reject you or judge your actions. Nobody is afraid to witness to a parked car — unless he thinks someone might be watching. If your assignment took you to a concealed car, there'd be nothing to it. Right? What does that tell us? When it comes to witnessing, **people scare people**. No one fears a parked car. But witnessing to a live person is another matter. Am I citing the obvious? There's a lesson here.

Do I really mean for you to approach a parked car? No. That assignment is for your imagination. I want you to visualize your feelings as you see yourself approaching a parked car and then a stranger. Can you "feel" the difference? The difference is THREAT — ego threat. It is the FEAR of people that silences witnesses. Therefore, this FEAR has to be dealt with. Any plan for producing witnesses must develop STRENGTHS which overcome the fear of man.

When we ask people to go into action for Jesus, we must deal with this FEAR. It is unrealistic to suppose it doesn't exist. It does. It has been silencing God's servants for centuries. Our plan for activating Christians assumes they are afraid to talk to people about Jesus. When we consider our objective: people joyously bringing the invitation of Christ to souls within their private world, we encounter the GAP between what they are and what they must become.

BRIDGING THE GAP

Many visitors stop by PC. Usually they come to examine our helps for starting people on the witness life. The Holy Spirit has produced a successful method for bridging the GAP between the **silent life** of Christian theory and the **aggressive life** of reaching one's private world. This method **eases** people into action by helping them absorb ego threat (fear) one bite at a time. It pleases me to tell visitors how the Holy Spirit arranged for me to discover this method by...... "accident."

The accident.

One day a man stopped by. With him was his little boy. The boy brought along his ball. While the dad was inside examining some soul-winning tools, the boy played outside. Shortly he burst into the room:

"Daddy, my ball is on the roof!"

You know kids. Somehow that ball got up there by itself.

A ladder makes an impossible task easy.

Well, everything had to stop until we recovered that ball. The dad thought it would be easy. He leaped atop a fence adjacent to the building, thinking to hoist himself to the roof. But it was too high. He couldn't quite make it. After repeated attempts he called to me:

"Don't you have a ladder around here some place?"

There was one in the back of the warehouse. We leaned it against the building. The dad quickly scrambled up and retrieved the ball from the roof. It was over in a couple of minutes.

"Of course!" I said that aloud. The father turned, he thought I was speaking to him. The Holy Spirit had just spoken to my spirit. I was so impressed the response came out vocally. For over eight months I had been asking the Spirit of God to show me a way to EASE Christians out of the pews and into action. I was having trouble with that GAP. I had been teaching the **Encounter-method** of soul-winning in churches all over the country, but getting

few soul-winners. It had me baffled. People were learning the plan, but few soul-winners were forthcoming.

Now there was nothing wrong with the method. It is extremely successful. Anyone who wants to win souls, can use it with terrific results. That's to be expected. The plan is based on the Holy Spirit Himself. The problem apparently lay in another direction. People were learning the skill, but **lacked** the STRENGTH to use it. This had to be the real problem. We can transfer the skill to a person with six hours of lab-work. In fact, he can stand before a group afterwards and demonstrate exactly how to lead a soul to Christ. So the problem **was not** a matter of skill. It had to be one of STRENGTH. For some time I had been asking the Lord for an answer when this man showed up.

That father was used of the Spirit to show me God's answer. Before my eyes the Lord demonstrated HOW to bridge the gap. Obviously it was impossible for the man to recover the lad's ball by going from the GROUND TO THE ROOF in **one jump**. He just couldn't do it. But with the help of a ladder, which broke the same distance into easily handled steps, he covered that same distance effortlessly. As I watched that father ascend the ladder, rung by rung, I saw God's answer. My soul rejoiced in His wisdom. That is exactly what I needed to give God's people. . .A LADDER TO BRIDGE THE DISTANCE.

● All I had to do now was develop a PLAN for reducing the GAP between the **theory world** and the **action world** to small steps anyone could take. If each step could move a man a little higher up the ladder, he would soon reach the top. Thus, what he couldn't possibly do in ONE JUMP, he could with small convenient witnessing actions. If the first steps could be stripped of fear so that they offered no threat of any kind, even the most timid Christian could get started. Such a method would allow every child of God to reach his private world with an action, even if it were but a slight one. Doesn't everything have to start someplace?

THE LADDER METHOD

Was I excited? You bet. I couldn't wait to begin experimenting with the Holy Spirit. His surging fire ignited my enthusiasm! Finally He was able to penetrate my thick skull. A plan began to take shape. Soon it was smoothed out and perfected. Early tests with interested Christians revealed the Spirit of God had given us something remarkable for His people.

What makes it work?

To answer that, we journey to a gym. But do you seat yourself in a chair? There is no lecture. The instructor takes you around and shows you the equipment. Then he puts some light weights in your hands. He starts you off with EASY exercises. You work with those for a few days. He gradually increases the weight and length of time for the workouts. Some months later you can handle heavy weights and do strenuous exercises. The point? **You actually work**. The stress is added a little at a time. It isn't long before your body shows the effect. There are definite changes.

The same is true in moving from the theory world of church to the action world of witnessing. You start off with easy exercises, non-threatening actions. Then you tackle the harder ones. As you go from step to step, your **witnessing strengths** change noticeably. Even your spirit changes. Your confidence in the Holy Spirit rises. Your spiritual muscles begin to bulge as you go from one kind of witnessing action to another. As they harden, you find yourself doing more and more for the Lord.

But what are these strengths?

We've said that people scare people. If people are afraid of people, then the place to commence the action is AWAY from others. And then, in succeeding steps, **ease closer and closer**. That way the THREAT is increased, bit by bit. It works like adding more and more weight to the gym exercises. That word "threat" is a key to witnessing success. If we find a way to absorb (or overcome) it, we are soon able to witness for Christ with great joy. When we learn to handle threat, we triumph over fear. It follows that when a Christian learns to conquer his fear of others, he can move boldly into his private world for Christ.

> **NOTE:** Christian courage is not the absence of fear, but the conquest of it in the power of the Holy Spirit. There is no plan anywhere that cancels fear. The Lord has not provided for any cancellation of our problems, but victory over them as we learn to operate in His power. This applies as fully to witnessing as any other area in our lives. There is no short cut to victory.

Once you see how easy it is to get started as a witness, I think you'll be eager to try. The only way to prove what I say, is to SAMPLE the action. Test it for yourself. See if the Holy Spirit hasn't provided this for His people. I believe every Christian senses he **should be** doing more for Christ, including you. When you see how the Holy Spirit can use this PLAN to ease people into action, you will be eager to enter the competition. I am going to introduce you to the LADDER-METHOD by explaining and assigning one of the actions of the bottom rung — step 1. You owe it to yourself to try it. It costs you nothing.

ACTION KIT

Did you notice the "action kit" which came with this book? Inside is a folded chart. On the outside it reads: **"How to get started with the Ladder-Method of Witnessing."** Take it out and open to the inside. I'LL WAIT. Good. See the ladder extending from the bottom to the top of the sheet? Notice how it reaches from the SILENT LIFE to the ACTION LIFE? The distance between them is divided into ten steps. Across the page is a brief explanation for each step.

All ten of those steps are dealt with in another book titled, **"Witnessing Made Easy."** But you won't need that to do what I will require of you in this action. After you taste the thrill of this first step, you may wish to go on. That is up to you. For those who enjoy personal coaching, all ten of these steps are available in our correspondence course. Now, however, we are interested only in the FIRST RUNG of the ladder. I want you to see how easy it is to get started. And what fun it is to enter the competition for Christ. Who minds being a bond-slave when it finally turns out to be fun!

RUNG 1 You are about to place your foot on the bottom rung of the ladder. Look over the #1 explanation. It is very brief. But it is not as simple as it sounds. I am going to give you an assignment. And this time I am serious. I want you to carry out this action. If you follow my instructions, you will taste spiritual adventure. You will sample the thrill of obedience. After that, you will be more eager to reach your private world for Jesus.

ASSIGNMENT

Look inside the action kit again. Locate the tracts, "A Penny for Your Thoughts." Fold them in half. They are ready to go into your tract holder. This fits conveniently into your shirt pocket or purse. If you are reading this book in the evening, place the holder on your dresser. That way you will spot it as you dress in the morning. Be sure it is in your pocket when you leave the house for work.

ACTION

1 Stop at a gas station (or restaurant) which has a restroom which provides LOCKED PRIVACY. It must have a door which **locks you in**. Otherwise you will lack the strict privacy you need for this exercise. Enter the room. Lock the door behind you. Stand in the center of the room. Reach to your pocket for a tract. But don't take it out—not just yet.

Let your hand linger over your heart for a few seconds. Kerplump! Kerplump! Kerplump! Feel that accelerated beat! Your heart is racing! Why? You are in the place of fear. You are about to do something for Jesus. . .**in the world**. That is scary, even behind a locked door. See how frightening this is! There is no way to do this in a church. **It's not a place of fear.** If one is going to learn to conquer fear in the power of the Spirit, he has to be in the PLACE OF FEAR. Isn't that elementary?

2 Now draw the tract from your pocket. Hold it out to your side at arm's length. Look at it. See how it quivers? Your fear has been translated into something

Your pulse races — in the place of fear!

you can SEE. The trembling of your heart corresponds to the shaking of your fingers. That fluttering tract is YOUR FEAR out there where you can look at it. The more shy you are as a Christian, the more that tract will quake. But that is good. The greater the fear, the greater the victory at hand.

3 With your arm **still extended** bow your head. You are going to speak directly to the Holy Spirit, even as your hand trembles. Say to Him. . .aloud. . . . .

"God the Holy Spirit, behold my trembling heart and comfort me now!"

Just that much. Look at your hand. It is settling down. What do you feel? The presence of the COMFORTER. His presence is like armor. There is His nearness and warmth in your own spirit. God's Person settles about you as a shield. A boldness

The doctrine of the Holy Spirit becomes an experience!

comes upon you. He was waiting to be asked. Like anyone else, He doesn't like being taken for granted. But now you have asked. The Comforter has responded. No longer is He a **doctrine** of your church, He is your EXPERIENCE. You have **experienced Him** in the world. That's an important shift from theory to action.

NOTE: Most evangelicals own sound doctrine concerning the Holy Spirit, but meeting those doctrines in **action** can be a surprise. Some, firmly settled in the truths of God's Spirit might not recognize those truths **when they occur.** When a doctrine becomes an action, a person enjoys an **experience.** But until he has this experience, his doctrine must remain as theory only. It is therefore, one thing to believe in the Spirit as the Comforter, another to experience His COMFORT in Person. So it is with all of the Spirit's ministries.

4 Now swing your arm so that the tract heads toward a towel box or shelf. Then deposit the tract. It can be any place in full view of someone who might enter the room after you. As the tract leaves your fingers, say aloud... **"In the Name of the Lord Jesus Christ!"** That is for your benefit. I want you to have the thrill of Jesus' Name on your lips in a **public place,** even if it is done privately the first time. There's a sweet joy which goes with it. That joy and the Spirit's presence can make you wonder what delight awaits you in the next step. It is exciting to THRILL to the Holy Spirit's anointing in a public place.

His Name feels good on your lips.

5 Unlock the door. Leave the room. As you go, check your heart once more. See, there is JOY now. You feel it. In fact you are rather flush with overwhelming joy. Obedience brings blessing, even the tiniest steps. What you feel is God's own pleasure. God receives thrills too. You just handed Him one. Even though you have only done a first step of the ladder, it offers as much promise to God as it does to you. When He is pleased, He has a way of sending a "well done" to your heart. The pleasure of God is not only a doctrine either. You can experience it, too.

The slightest obedience brings great joy!

TOO TINY?

Does that little exercise seem overly simple to you? Perhaps a little ridiculous? I assure you it isn't. It is a major step into the ACTION-WORLD. More vital than many suspect. Did you know there are people winning souls today who have skipped this action. Most of them serve Christ out of a **sense of duty** rather than in the thrill of His power. To be a witness for Jesus, and **love every minute of it,** demands people have this acquaintance with God's Spirit. Those without it, must drive themselves. Those discovering the joy of this first step want more.

● No, the step is not insignificant. Let's take another look and see what really happens when you complete this assignment:

A You become acquainted with God's Spirit in **the world.** In the very place where the Great Commission sends you, you discover the Spirit ALIVE, eager to be your strength. A person actually experiences the COMFORTER at a time when fear is shaking a tract before his very eyes. This could **not be done** in a church or even a witnessing class. One must GO into the world to do this.

B By an experience, you find that FEAR can be overcome in the POWER of the Holy Spirit. It is not something read in a book, nor of someone else's testimony — it HAPPENS TO YOU! It is one thing for a Christian to read the lines: "Christian courage is not the absence of fear, but the conquest of it in the power of the Holy Spirit," something else to experience it.

C You enjoy **locked privacy.** Why? Unless you felt totally secure, your **mind** would be occupied with something else. . . . "What if someone came in and saw me doing this?" The **threat of discovery** would have been so great, it would have **numbed your spirit.** A person cannot observe God's working when external threat is too great. You see, even though the Spirit's presence is real, it is faint when a Christian is first getting acquainted with Him this way. The possibility of someone walking in on you, is enough to cancel your awareness of God's presence. That's why a secure situation, yet one which is in the world, is needed for the first action.

D It is no small thing to have Jesus' Name on your lips in a public place. A locked room provides a wonderful starting place. As your confidence grows, His Name comes to your lips more easily. Everybody who speaks out fearlessly for Christ had to begin somewhere. The easier we make that beginning, the more people we can activate for the Lord. If we can make it easy enough, every child of God can become outspoken for Christ, if he wants to.

The only reason he wouldn't, is because he **doesn't care** enough for Jesus to bother.

E Then there is the JOY that obedience brings. Once a man **tastes** God's "well done," in his soul, he craves more. There is an intoxication which goes with it. This inner joy makes a man a serious contender for a good job with Jesus. Ah, but there's another lesson in this experience. If obedience brings blessing, then disobedience means the **absence** of God's blessing. What of all those who are "hearers only?" Doesn't this explain the **sad looks** on Christian faces today? Where there is no obedience, God cannot send blessing. He cannot bless disobedience.

F Then there's the actual witness itself. The tract is left in a public crossroad. You leave it, that's all. The Holy Spirit engineers the results. He sees that it gets into the hands of the right person. The hidden-tract method is unique in this respect. People can be reached this way, who **cannot be reached** any other. You don't know who will pick it up. Long after you are gone, the Spirit matches the tract with the right prospect. There are souls who will not visit a church, listen to Gospel radio or TV, or talk with a witness. But they will **secretly read a tract.** Step #1 of the Ladder-method lets you reach them. There is **no other ministry** which duplicates this action. See how easy it is to start reaching your private world? (Matt. 13:44).

WOULD YOU DO THAT MUCH?

I have set before you a simple action in the world. I consider it the irreducible minimum of Christian action outside the church. How much effort does it take? You go to the gas station anyway. Why not pause in the restroom for a few seconds? That's all it takes. You eat out once in awhile? Then why not see if the restroom is fully private. Carry the tract on your person and conduct this experiment as a part of your ordinary routine. It won't even take you out of your way. Then see if the Lord doesn't send His "well done" to your soul.

But if you won't do that much for Jesus, what can you say to yourself about calling Him Lord? What do thoughts of the judgment do to you in that case? If you won't stir yourself to try a simple step of obedience, such as this — should you continue thinking of Jesus as your Lord? Those are bitter words, I know. I hate to talk like that, but I must — even if only for a few lines.

I prefer to think you are weighing my words and checking for the Spirit's witness. I'd rather believe you long to please God, yearning to do His will. If that's the case, let me ask. . . . **"Do you think there is more to be had in Christ, than you are experiencing today?"**

Dear reader, I have had the joy of witnessing for Jesus for some years now. I can testify that there are pleasures to be had, thrills to enjoy. Nothing I know of, equals the heart-pounding excitement of **moving** in the power of God! I find this to be our Christian birthright. Those who settle for less, live way below their privileges in Christ. Even worse, they are missing the best of their own faith.

Wouldn't you hate to think that what we find in Churchianity today is the best God has for His people? You're not ready to settle for that are you? Don't you sense there is more — a lot more? Sure you do. And I want you to have it. Once you sample the real thrill of Christ you'll agree that a world of adventure beckons.

TASTE AND SEE!

Serve Christ **in the Spirit,** and your soul explodes with a new kind of living! The world has nothing to match such thrills. I mean it when I assign the "locked-privacy" experiment. I want you to take that tract to a public place and **prove** the Spirit of God. You can't imagine how much I mean it. Were I there with you right now, I'd extend my hand, coaxing you to rise from your chair. I'd say. . . .

> "Come. Let's go together. I'll show you how exciting it is to operate in the power of the Holy Spirit. I'll prove to you, you can taste that 'well done' right now!"

Then we'd go — afterwards to find our hearts pounding with delight. You'd be so excited you wouldn't want to return home. It's like dope, dear reader, this privilege of moving in power. Taste it once and you want more.

There are lots of windshield wipers waiting to receive tracts...

and lots of phone booths, too.

Now there is no way to sit there reading a book and know about power. You can't make such judgments on the basis of theory. You must **SAMPLE** the anointing, you must taste it. But isn't that the formula of Christianity? Everything God offers is on that basis — even Jesus Himself... **"Taste and see that the Lord is good."*** So with the thrill of moving in His power. There is no way to speculate about such adventure. No one can know the joy of witnessing in the Spirit **until he tries**. That's why I urge you sample the action I have assigned.

Here's a lady who sampled. . . . .**

Dear CS: Praise God for Personal Christianity. Never have I been so excited about serving the Lord and pointing the way for other Christians to do likewise. In the past, my husband and I have had several of your books. But a short time ago, the Holy Spirit led me to pick up **Witnessing Made Easy.** The timing was just right.

I was so fascinated by the way it met the need in my life, I couldn't put it down. I started to use the plan, going up the ladder as you outlined. The Lord has allowed me to see some marvelous results. Also I am going to take the correspondence course and teach these steps to a class of interested women. I am simply bubbling over with joy and I want to share it with others. Thank you for your wonderful ministry. May God continue to bless you.

Sincerely, in Christ,

Marilyn Hall
507 E. 7th St.
Wellston OH 45692

SO CHANGE YOUR LIFE

Trade the easy ways of American living and submit to Christ Jesus. You won't be sorry. Be His servant night and day and live in the pleasure of His praise. Put His interests above your own. Spend yourself for Him and thrill to the power that comes with being His agent in this world! There

---
*Psalm 34:8
**I have Mrs. Hall's permission to quote from her letter.

is no greater privilege! Put everything behind you and reach for the prize! Let nothing hinder you, neither family, fortune nor fame. Do it while you still have time.

THEN — when death strikes your body

You will have absolutely NO TERROR of the judgment. The Apostle Paul reached the place where he could say.. **"For me to live is Christ, to die is GAIN!"** Do as I suggest and you will feel the same way. You will appear before the bar of God with a smile on your face. As you look into the face of your Saviour and JUDGE, He will be SMILING TOO! That would be glory enough, but then comes the exultation of your soul...

"Well done thou good and faithful servant!
Enter thou into the joy of thy Lord!"

Oh happy day! You embrace eternity with a shout! You have served Christ to reap an eternity of rank and royalty. That's not bad for someone who is just....

... A SERVANT!

The joy of Christ's servants is eternal!

NOW THEN . . .

You've read the book. Look again at the tract I asked you to take to a locked restroom. Hold it in your fingers. I am satisfied the Spirit is prompting you to experiment with Him. I consider the assignment I gave in Chapter Five to be the irreducible minimum of Christian **action**. Why would a person refuse to carry out such a simple step for Christ? The only reason I can think of is — **he doesn't want to**. Not because he couldn't. The person who won't do that much for Jesus should soberly ask himself. . **"Do I really care about the Lord at all? Do I wish only to take from Him, giving back nothing in return?"** To me it is unthinkable that a person could really care and refuse this slight bit of obedience.

As you read these lines, I know He is not only bearing witness but challenging you to action. Try the experiment.Once you do,I'm sure you'll want to join the competition. Give yourself the "shake-test" in locked privacy. You'll thrill to the engulfing presence of the Spirit. You can't help but want more. Give Him a chance to deal with your FEAR and you will want to try the harder steps for the pure adventure of it. No one can enjoy such a taste and not want more.

It would be cruel of me to leave you panting for more of God's anointing and say nothing of the next steps. It would be heartless to give this delightful sample, which is only part of rung I, and not tell you how to reach for more. Therefore I am obliged to mention the correspondence course. It is my business to help those who long to be near the Lord in eternity. There is no way to experience God's power in a classroom. The **mechanics of moving** in the Spirit cannot be taught that way. Therefore I owe it to you to speak of this plan which eases Christians into action in their private worlds.

The correspondence course.

Again open the large chart from the action-kit. See the ten rungs of the ladder, and how they lift a man from the

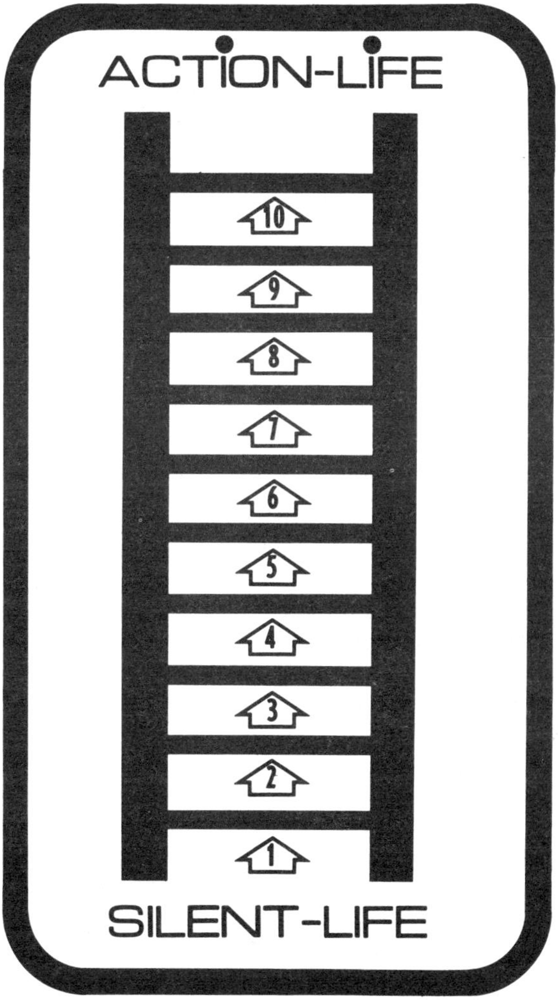

Becoming a witness is easier — one step at a time.

silent-life to the action-life in Christ. The details provided across the page are very scant. There is considerable action for each step. All ten have been developed as a correspondence course. I am the teacher. Each of these rungs is a separate lesson. Each equips you with a bit more skill. As you advance up the ladder you meet more threat. But you learn to overcome your fears in the power of the Spirit before advancing to the next step.

● You do not receive all ten lessons at once. You start off with two. That way you have one to work on, while the other is in the mail. You carry out specific action-assignments. You make action reports. As soon as I receive an action report, the next lesson is mailed.

How to get started.

There are three things to do to enroll in the course:

1. Take the application from the kit. Read it and fill it out. Sign it. From the information on this application a permanent record is made for you here at PC headquarters and a chart is used to plot your progress.

2. Sit down and write a letter to me telling how you KNOW you are saved. I want you to put your salvation experience on paper. To do so, ask yourself . . . **"What right do I have to call myself a born-again Christian?"** Think too about the ways you reassure yourself you are safe in the Lord. Put it all on paper, describing the best you can the mechanics of your surety in Christ. It doesn't have to be long, just factual. I am not interested in your spelling or handwriting.

Don't try to satisfy me with your statement, satisfy yourself.

This action is not as simple as it sounds. To put things of this nature on paper, a person must first process them in his mind. It often takes a lot of mental energy to reshape scattered and unfocused ideas into a solid statement, but that's what I want. If your experience in Christ is vague and shadowy, this can be a rewarding assignment. The witness-life requires a firm base. It is the launching pad from which you will go into orbit, so it must be solid.

3. Along with your application and salvation letter, enclose the enrollment fee—$10.00. You will understand this is not a money making venture when I tell you the cost of the materials for this course runs $8.38. Handling and lesson grading is not a part of that total. The purpose of this course is solely to activate saints for Christ, with the confidence that our "profit" will be laid up and waiting for the day when we will see you there!

Here are the advantages of climbing the witnessing ladder this way:

- Your work is more determined and systematic with the discipline of accounting to someone else, as reinforced by the heart-treasure principle when you invest the $10.00.
- If you are a pastor or teacher, you can systematically bring your people along a step or two behind you. You can put the know-how to work in your group even as you ascend the 10 rungs of the ladder.
- Each time we receive an action report, you receive a prayer-boost by name as your report goes before the Friday night prayer-band.
- If you begin to show excessive lag in your reporting, a follow-up letter will spur you on to increased dedication.
- You receive a membership card and **permanent number** when you reach the fifth rung of the ladder. This number can be used to earn an **immediate discount** on all supplies you order from PC. In time this can return the cost of the course.
- Upon completion of the course, you receive the silver PC pin. These coveted pins are kept locked in a safe, and there is no way to secure one except by completing all ten action steps of the witnessing ladder. They truly certify the wearer to be an active and skilled witness for Christ.
- You can take your time. Some take as long as one year to complete the course. The fastest is three months. You advance to the next higher rung after you have learned to be **comfortable** witnessing at the lower level. The pressure is your own ambition to go as far as you can in Christ.

SO DO IT

Go to the place where you do your letter writing. Take pen and paper and get your salvation experience down in black and white. You'll enjoy the sweet exhilaration doing just that much. The thrill of entering the competition will create early excitement in your life. But don't wait. Satan will try to get you to put this off. Tell him to beat it! You will be stirred to action if you remember my challenge. . . .

JESUS IS COMING—GET READY CHRISTIAN!

HAS THIS BOOK HELPED YOU.........?

If you feel **"Jesus Is Coming...!"** has alerted you to "your last enemy," surely there are brethren about you who also need this warning counsel. When a Christian discovers something of unusual blessing, he has an obligation to share it with others in the body of Christ.

A tract has been developed which makes it easy to do just that. In the action kit you will find copies of **"Your last enemy!"** It is simple to use. Picture yourself at church next Sunday, or the prayer meeting. A brother or sister approaches to inquire...."How are you today?" A sly Christian answer would be...

"I'm better now, thank you."

"Oh, have you been ill?"

"No, but ever since I found out about our last enemy, I FEEL BETTER about meeting him. I'd feel even better if you knew about him!"

"What do you mean? What enemy?"

"Here, read this. It will tell you about him."

As soon as you get a copy of this tract in another Christians hands, the Holy Spirit will take it from there. Even more powerfully if you are praying that instant. The Spirit will press His own warning and urgency with those lines. He may even cause questions to reach the person's mind. Should your Christian friend show real interest, offer to loan him your book. If the Lord uses you to activate a Christian brother or sister in this fashion, your own wealth in Christ will be enhanced.

HINT: Arrive at the Sunday school class room a little early. Put a copy of this tract on each of the chairs. The students will find them when they come in. In moments, the room will buzz with comment. Who knows, you might be used of God to bring a discussion on the finality of the Christian life. In that case, a number of people might go into action and your "override" would be greater still. This is perhaps the most successful "Get-rich-quick" scheme in Christianity. We speak of spiritual riches, of course. And you know this hint is not a substitute for reaching your own private world. If you need more tracts, **"Your last enemy!"** is available free of charge from Personal Christianity.

A witnessing course application placed in a brother's hands could get another Christian into action!

APPENDIX . . .

THE JUDGE'S YARDSTICK*

Remember those six-weeks and mid-term exams we had in school? How we groaned as we faced those quizzes. Yet they helped us. They let us know how we were doing. We could pour on the coal and improve our grades if we had to.

Unfortunately there are no midterms in Christian service. God lets us go all through our earthly lives and then. . . .

THE FINAL EXAM!

That's what the judgment is to the Christian — **his final exam**. The Judge's evaluation appears on the eternal report card. The grades stand forever. No one can return to earth thinking to improve his grade. Those marks are indelible, showing how well or poorly a servant has executed his stewardship. Those grades are his forever!

THE JUDGE'S YARDSTICK

Wondering how the Judge evaluates each servant, what He uses for a measuring stick? It is important to know what counts with Christ. He has given considerable teaching as to what He expects of His servants. I have selected four of His parables which mark the different things He looks for in His servants.

Parables?

Our Lord was an amazing teacher. The parable was His favorite device for putting across truths. A parable is a truth clothed in a familiar illustration. He took things from the daily lives of His listeners and used them as vehicles of communication. People in that day had no difficulty understanding what He meant. But alas, we live in another day. Customs and habits are different, the circumstances centuries old. So everything has to be explained. What was a simple tool then, is sometimes an awkward device for us. Even so the truth is there for us to uncover and receive.

*Exposition of parables mentioned on page 44.

PARABLE No. 1 LUKE 16:1-13

Teaching: The WISDOM of a servant in considering his future and doing what he can to provide for himself after his stewardship ends.

The parable tells of a business manager who was careless in handling his employer's estate. When the owner learned of it, he called the manager to his office and gave him his dismissal notice. Realizing his future was in danger, with but a short time left in his job, he resorted to scheming. One by one he sought out his master's debtors and had them change their invoices to show they owed far less than they really did. In this way he made himself friends of those debtors. He assumed they would be pleased to return the favor when he was finally out of a job.

Jesus said that when the master heard of his steward's strategy, he didn't get angry. Instead he praised his steward for being clever and wise enough to look out for himself. Then the Lord Jesus drew a comparison between this fore-sighted servant and His own servants:

> "For the sons of this age (non-Christians) are more shrewd in relation to their own kind, than the sons of light" (Luke 16:8b).

● Note the desperation of this steward as he was about to lose his job. See how he moved to do what was necessary in providing for his future? We observe the Lord Jesus was NOT teaching this man was wise in resorting to dishonesty. The point of the parable deals with wisdom in **thinking about his future,** and **doing something about it**. The application is obvious: **we know we will one day be out of our earthly stewardships, and should be wisely feathering our nests in heaven.**

Just as that manager used his master's goods to win favor with the debtors, we should use this world's opportunity and treasure to secure our future position in heaven. Since the Lord bought us, our time and money are not really ours, but His. Yet we can use them to advance our future status. When we do, we show the same wisdom as the steward in the parable. That is why the Lord told it. This was His teaching. That it is the correct interpretation we know, for the Lord didn't stop there.

"And I say to you (Christians) make friends for yourselves (future friends) by means of the mammon of unrighteousness (earthly wealth), so that when it (your earthly stewardship) fails; they may receive you into the eternal dwellings" (Vs. 9).

Who receives us? Those whom we have made our friends through the use of mammon. And who might that be? Converts for Christ, plus all those we reach and help in Jesus' Name. The Lord is counseling us to use every possible means to advance our fortunes in heaven. We are to be as "WISE" as that manager in using this world's goods to enhance our future position with Him. Money is time and talent in negotiable form. So He asks us to use money or "mammon" in His service rather than squandering it foolishly on "things" in this world.

Dr. Oswald J. Smith says it runs about 14¢ per person to bring a soul to Christ via literature, but $100,000.00 per soul by the usual church-method. That could be something to think about when exercising shrewdness about your future.

PARABLE No. 2 **MATTHEW 25:14-30**

Teaching: How the Lord compensates a servant for his FAITHFULNESS to his own task, without regard for the opportunities given to other Christians.

This time the Lord Jesus tells of a well-to-do man about to embark on a journey. Before he leaves, he calls his servants and distributes **varying sums** to each. They are required to use the money so as to make more for him while he is away. Apparently the master knew his servants quite well, for the amounts given to each were based on their ability to handle money. The amount matched each man's financial skill.

As soon as the master left, his servants got busy. The man who received five talents (about $5,000, we'll say), negotiated to earn another $5000. The one who had received the two talents ($2000), earned $2000 more. But alas, the one who had received the single talent ($1000), did nothing with his master's money. **He didn't even try**. He merely hid it in a safe place ready to hand back on his master's return. Then he proceeded to go about his **own** business, totally indifferent to what he had been commissioned to do.

The rich man returned. He called his servants before him, asking for their reports. Each had to account for how he had fared investing the master's money.

The first servant joyfully reported he had doubled what was given him. The master was delighted. He promised his servant would be trusted with far greater responsibility in the future. The second slave had the same report. He too had doubled his master's money. Though he had less to start with, his **reward was identical** to that of the servant with the $5000. He too was promised greater responsibility. His reward was NO DIFFERENT from the man with the greater opportunity. And that is the point of the parable.

When you read this account in the Testament, you will see how this parable teaches that FAITHFULNESS to the task — even though abilities and opportunities differ — brings exactly the **same reward**. Not all of God's people are gifted the same, therefore not all do the same work for Jesus. BUT. . . all can be **faithful** with what they have. All can fulfill the task assigned to them. This is what the Master requires.

See how the recompense is NOT based on what someone else does? You and I are responsible only for what God gives **us** to do. Our eyes, therefore, should rest on our **own** task. What some other Christian does or is able to do, does NOT affect our reward in the slightest. This is what the JUDGE teaches by this parable.

● Now we come to the third man. No doubt there were other servants, but the Holy Spirit gives three examples as representative of the situation. This man received less than any of the others, only $1000. All he had to do was earn an additional $1000 and he would receive the same reward as the others. If he demonstrated the **same faithfulness** his reward would be equal to the rest. But what did he do?

Nothing. He ignored both his opportunity and responsibility. It mattered not that he was **told** to USE the money. He busied himself with what he pleased, indifferent to his master's instruction. He selfishly went about his own interests, caring not that his owner trusted him. There is no question as to who came first with him. Doesn't he remind you of "the man who teases Jesus?" Let's see how he reacts when called to account. Here's his report:

> "I knew you were a hard businessman, expecting to profit even though you do no actual work. It is clear that you make gains off of what others do. Well, I was afraid of your severity. So I decided not to risk your money on investments. Instead, I kept it safe for you, so that it would be here waiting for you when you got back."

Listen to that, would you? He pretends to care about his master's interest. But we know he doesn't. Neither does he have any respect for his master. He wouldn't dare take him to task for being an investor rather than a laborer, if he did. Impudently he suggests his master has no right to expect any profit from him at all. If he really cared for his lord, he would have made some effort to bring him a profit.

What a wicked fellow he is. He lies. The truth is, he simply couldn't be bothered. Notice he says he fears his master as a "hard man?" That's a lie, too. He thinks his master is a softie, otherwise how could he expect to get away with such impudence. He expects to get away with it. That's obvious.

Recognize any Christians like that? **"God is a good God,"** some say. **"He won't deal harshly with His own servants, even if they fail to fulfill their assignments."** Consequently they forget His commission, to live as they please. They are just like this servant. They put their own interests first, thinking it doesn't matter that the Lord has assigned them a job. It is a low estimate of Jesus that expects Him to be satisfied with disobedience. Why should He expect less than any other master?

A Christian who does not fear God's judgment is a fool. Pity those who shrug off their responsibility to Christ. What a surprise they will have when He calls them to account. Let's see what awaited the servant who thought his master would wink at his indifference. He's in for a shock:

"You wicked and lazy servant! If you really believed that I was a hard man, you would have at least put my money in the bank to let it draw depositor's interest. But no, you wouldn't even bother to do that!"

Wow! His master sees right through him! He calls him wicked as well as lazy. The very least he should have done was to take the trouble of earning bank interest for his master. Even though he feared to speculate with it, he could have put it in the bank. He obviously despised both his master and his commission, expecting to get away with the whole business by means of an excuse. I hope no one who reads this book plans to try that on the Lord in the judgment. He will see right through it.

The servant's excuse didn't work:

"Therefore take away the talent he has and give it to the one with the ten . . . and throw him into outer darkness—in that place where is weeping and wailing and gnashing of teeth" (Vs. 30).

NOTE: See the different degrees of anguish? The weeping is less intense than the wail. The wail less intense than the rage which makes a man gnash his teeth. All, of course are personal torments. Not every servant will suffer the same. Some may accept what comes, sad that they didn't prosecute their privileges. Others will be sick at heart. Still more will be furious with themselves. Unfortunately there are no second chances. Our master is not going away a second time.

Whew! he never expected to hear that. He miscalculated his master. His lord is a JUST man, as faithful to hand out **consequences** as he is to **reward** those who obey. Do you suppose if this servant had truly known his master, he would have dared to be so callous with his commission? He got into trouble because he **didn't know his master** as he should have. He thought he knew him. He was sure he had sized him up correctly and could get away with this. But he didn't. How many Christians are mis-judging the Lord Jesus the same way? They're going to be horrified to discover their mistake — too late!

Now do I hear another protest:

> "Hey! We're blood bought Christians. We're the Lord's own brethren, children of God. How is it possible, even thinkable, that we could expect harsh treatment at the hand of the Lord? Surely Someone Who loves us enough to die for us wouldn't deal with us so severely!"

That protest isn't too different from the one we've been hearing all along. People just can't bring themselves to believe God is JUST. They expect His love to **overlook evil** in them. What a surprise awaits those with this low estimate of the Lord. Honestly, though, are these words really any stronger than:

"Draw back from Him in shame!" (1 John 2:28).

It's the same idea. Why should Christians shrink from Christ, if not because they have failed to honor Him as LORD? That's the only reason why any should tremble at His sight. We rightly fear judgment when we refuse to serve Him as Master. Anyone who ignores the interest of his Lord, can expect to be treated as a wicked servant. No trick of theology can alter this hard fact. Those who feel as did this servant, cannot avoid the consequences.

- But someone else says:

"This parable has to do with the unsaved!"

Hardly. The man is going on a journey, expecting to return. Who will say that the Lord Jesus is not referring to Himself? The man calls his **own servants.** He gives them tasks while he is away. Can this be anything other than the commission assigned to God's people? The CONTEXT is faithfulness to one's master. It is difficult to see how these could be other than Christ's own.

It would be a serious distortion to apply this to non-Christians. On the surface, at least, it has to do with REWARDING people for FAITHFULNESS to an **assigned job**. Of course, I can be wrong. I never seek to impose my own views on others. The Holy Spirit will have to umpire the matter. He is the final authority, the only dependable witness. Besides, other parables shed more light on this question.

The return banquet.

Meanwhile, back at the parable. More action is taking place. It's time for a party. It was the custom in the East, to hold such a party upon the landlord's return. More so when his prosperity is increased at the hands of his faithful servants. When a man's servants added to his wealth, it was the custom to have a celebration and let them share in the joy of it. From my tour of duty in India, I remember it took much less than this to warrant a party. Now here's the way the rich man worded his invitation. . . . .

"Enter thou into the joy of your master."

That invitation meant they were to join him at his table. Servants never do this unless bidden. When a slave was asked to sit at his master's table, it amounted to a tremendous elevation. I am thinking of my numerous visits to Indian homes. The servants were not even allowed to stand **near** the table, let alone be seated as friends.

What of the wicked servant?

The disobedient slave had his one talent taken away. Never again would he invest for his master. Never would he be able to recover from his blunder. His talent was given to someone who could easily handle it, the man with the ten. The faithless man has proven himself unfit. What's to become of him?

For one thing, he is not allowed in the banquet room. He is not even to have the privilege of waiting on the table. Is he still a servant? Yes. His master still owns him. But instead of being elevated, he is humiliated. He suffers embarrassment and loss of rank. He isn't even allowed in the house, so as to enjoy the light.

Banquets of this sort were always held at night. The halls were lighted by oil lamps. Outside it is dark. Some Eastern nights are pitch black. So into the darkness he goes, away from the light and festivities. The closest he can come is to observe the celebration through a window. As he sees his former companions enjoying themselves, listening to the happy sound of the master's voice, he could kick himself. He grinds his teeth as he thinks how he might have been soaking in the pleasure of the occasion.

But he isn't alone out there. There are others, also unfaithful. With this group he must now be content. All of them will be upset to one degree or another. All have forfeited friendship with the master and a place at his table. But perhaps our man is the most miserable. He had the easiest job of all. Therefore he will be the hardest on himself. Some around him will be weeping, others will voice self-pity, our servant here, will be grinding his teeth in rage. People are maddest when they cause their own downfall.

> **WARNING:** Those spurning their stewardship in Christ will NOT enter into the joy of the faithful. Yes, they will be in heaven. The Lord is faithful even to His worst slaves. They are fickle, He is not. He will never cast away anyone who comes to Him, even though the consequences of disobedience are bitter. The Lord will yet use them. After all, He is a genius. He will have jobs for the unfaithful. Jobs which match their personalities and disposition. Romans 8:28 applies to heaven too. We can expect these bitterly disappointed people to fill useful roles in glory. Of course, it will be a far cry from what they could have enjoyed had they elected to live for Christ instead of themselves.

The reason I give this warning is to prepare you for Jesus' words spoken **after** He finished the parable. He made an application. It is not a part of the story, but the penetrating truth of what that story means to you and me:

> **"For to everyone who has, shall more be given, and he shall have abundance; but from the one who does not have, even that which he has shall be taken away"** (Vs. 29).

Taken away?

That, dear reader, is a sobering truth. Did you ever dream that something you had in Christ, could be taken away? Remember the word. . . .LOSS? Paul used it in his warning of the Judgment Seat. Yes, it is possible to LOSE much in Christ. Have you heard the counsel which the Lord Jesus spoke through His servant John:

> **"Behold I come quickly; hold fast that which you have, that no man take thy crown"** (Rev. 3:11).

That warning was given to the church at Philadelphia, regarded by scholars as representing the true ones in Christ. That word for **crown** in Greek, means a REWARD secured by participating in competition. What is important to us is to see that it is something which can be LOST. May not any race be won or lost? If we don't think we can lose in the Christian contest, we'd better review our theology. Our doctrine might be lulling us to sleep, making us careless. It is foolish to assume you have won something — when you haven't.

Before us now are Jesus' words which speak of the LOSS of reward. Once something is taken away, as in the case of the servant, all hope of recovery is gone. There is nothing a person can do to improve his situation after the opportunity passes from his hands. The meaning is clear: if we as Christians, throw away the opportunity we have to serve Christ in this life, the LOSS we will suffer at the judgment, is irretrievable. That is the sober side of salvation.

Perhaps now someone is ready to warn me: **"Aren't you building a lot on one parable, Brother Lovett?"** That's fair. It is risky to build too heavily on a single passage of Scripture. What we will do then, is go to another parable. If what I have set forth is true, that truth should appear often in the Word of God. Any single truth of God's Word should be consistent with the sum. Let's see if we're right.

PARABLE 3 **LUKE 19:11-27**

Teaching: How the Lord compensates servants manifesting DIFFERENT DEGREES of faithfulness in the SAME opportunity.

Dr. Luke tells us the Lord gave this parable because His listeners thought the Kingdom of God was about to appear. Consequently it has to do with the DELAY of His kingdom and what was to happen in the meantime. While the setting is a little different, the story is similar to the parable of the talents. This one is often referred to as the parable of the pounds, but that is inaccurate. It is more properly called the

Parable of the Mina.

This time the story is about a high ranking nobleman who had apparently rendered a great service to his emperor and was invited to the capital to have a kingdom conferred upon him. (The story is meaningful to Jesus' listeners. Such a thing had actually happened and was a part of recent Palestine history.) Before departing, the nobleman summoned his ten slaves before him. He gave each one mina (about $20.00), instructing him to do business with it while he was gone. When he returned, he called them to give an account of what they had done with the $20.00.

OBSERVE: The stewardship in this case is very slight, for the mina ($20.00) is nowhere near the value of the talent ($1,000.00). In this case, each man is given the SAME. The parable therefore is dealing with **faithfulness** in a matter of small value, rather than one of extreme value, doubtless applying to something all Christians have in common.

On the surface, the accounting scene resembles the one in Matthew. But the reports are quite different. Since each man has a single mina to invest, all have the SAME opportunity. The first man steps up proudly. He holds out to his master ten minas more. He has produced 10 times over for his lord. The master beams:

"Well done, good slave, because you have been faithful in very little, be in authority over TEN cities" (Vs. 17).

NOTE: The kingdom which the master received would no doubt include numerous cities. Even as Jesus was speaking, certain cities of Palestine belonged to different Roman rulers. Herod the Great, for example, had given four cities to his sister Salome. Usually it was done to provide favored persons with income and prestige. In the story, the master is now delegating positions to servants within the newly received kingdom. Imagine receiving 10 cities, because one had been faithful to multiply a $20 bill! That is staggering, but it represents the generosity of our Lord Jesus! Those who are faithful in little things will be shocked to see the great reward it brings.

Then the next man stepped up to account for what he had done with his mina. Consider again that he had exactly the same opportunity as the man before him. But he brings his master only FIVE minas. Still, he is rewarded:

"You are to be over five cities."

NOTE: The "Well done" is **missing.** He doesn't deserve the **same commendation,** his effort has been less. Yet he is rewarded according to his faithfulness—he receives FIVE cities. We observe now that the one who **does the most** with what he has, **profits most** in the accounting. Even so, **anything gained** through obedience to the master earns a reward.

Every slave had the same chance to qualify. None was disadvantaged, none was privileged. The opportunity for each was **unlimited.** That wasn't the case in the parable of the talents where each was portioned **"according to his ability."** But in this parable of the mina, every man starts off the same. All are in the same category. The variable is the **industriousness** with which each applies himself. While all have the same opportunity, not all work with the same zeal and determination.

● Now to see what happened to the third fellow. (Again, these three are only representative of the many servants the man had.) If we have mis-handled the truth of consequences, perhaps any error will show up here. Here he comes. I don't see a smile on his face. He doesn't appear eager to give his report. His story isn't too different from the one who hid his master's money in the ground:

"Master, here's your mina. I kept it safe for you, right here in this handkerchief. (Can you see him unfolding it?) I was afraid of you, for I know how hard and exacting you are. You make money without working for it. You take up what you don't lay down, you reap what you don't sow. I know how you expect to make a profit off of everything and everybody. So, knowing how you feel, I felt it would be better not to risk your money. Here it is, all safe and sound."

Oops. He would have been better off if he hadn't said that. For not only did he fail to obey his master, he also indicts him for severity. But he lies, of course. Had he really believed his master to be tough, he **wouldn't dare** disobey him. The truth is, he regarded his master a pushover for a sad story. But he condemned himself with his own words. The master saw through him at once. If he had any fear of his master at all, he never would have allowed that $20 to remain idle. His master confronts him with his contradiction:

> **"Out of thine own mouth will I judge you, you wicked servant. . . . If you knew me to be such a hard man, why didn't you put my money in the bank, so that when I got back I could at least have the interest on it?"** (Vss. 22-23).

Ah, the truth was, the man didn't care. He didn't bother himself with his master's orders. He went his own way. He remained indifferent to what his master required of him. But he didn't get away with it. As in the case of his counterpart, in the parable of the talents, he too lost what he once had. He came to the end of his opportunity. No longer did he have a mina to use for his master.

> **"Take the mina away from him," said the master, "and give it to the one who has ten"** (Vs. 24).

The wicked servant suffered the LOSS of his mina, his opportunity. That meant he forfeited **forever** the privilege of earning a place in his master's kingdom. He received no cities. He lost the privilege of competing for any. He was absolutely through qualifying as a faithful servant. There can be no cities for him — **ever**. He will never reign with his master.

With the story concluded, the Lord Jesus presses the application upon His disciples:

> **"I tell you, that to everyone who has shall more be given, but from the one who does not have (through neglect or disobedience), even that which he has shall be taken away!"** (Vs. 26).

Just as the servant in the story suffered LOSS, so will the children of God if they allow themselves to fall into a similar attitude. The SAME LOSS will occur at the Judgment Seat for those refusing to invest in Christ. While the servant LOST forever what he could have had through faithfulness, he still REMAINED the servant of his master. **Don't miss that.** The LOSS we speak of here is not salvation, but the REWARD of faithfulness. The opportunity for that **reward** ends when the Master calls us to account.

● Now this parable DOES speak of the unsaved. Some **verses are added** which pertain to them. But notice they are NOT called servants, but **enemies.** See how differently they are treated:

> **"Bring those enemies (not servants) of mine, who did not want me to reign over them here before me and slay them in my presence"** (Vs. 27).

The enemies of God are those outside of Christ (Rom. 5:10). The servants of the Lord are not regarded as enemies. We have already observed that:

> **"Ye are My friends if ye do whatsoever I command you"** (John 15:14).

See what awaits those outside of Christ — DEATH — eternal death. A faithless servant might be expelled from the lighted hall into outer darkness of the work areas, but he is **not slain.** It would be a horrible distortion of the Gospel to hint that even the most wretched child of God would finally suffer spiritual death. That is contrary to the invitation: **"He that cometh unto Me I will in no wise cast out"** (John 6:37). We must distinguish between those who refuse Christ as Saviour and those who refuse Him as **LORD**. The Saviourhood of Jesus and His Lordship are separate matters. He is both Saviour and Lord.

There are those who own Christ Jesus as Saviour, but deny His Lordship over their lives. They reach heaven all right. But when they try to hand Him back their fruitless lives neatly wrapped in the handkerchief of disobedience, it will be a miserable moment. They will hear no "Well done." They will receive **no** reward. They will LOSE the **opportunity to qualify** for any position of authority in His kingdom. Faithless servants of the Lord will not like what they hear at the judgment.

Who's to blame? The Master? No. He has given every Christian a mina. Likely the broadest interpretation we can give the mina is to let it represent our one life to live for Christ. There may be narrower, more specific definitions, but we'll stay with the wider one. It's safer, theologically. Every Christian has one life to live for Christ. There is no limit to how far a man can press that one opportunity. The only limitation is his personal zeal and ambition.

Do we actually reign with Christ?

While the story speaks of cities appointed to the faithful servants, can we go so far as to think that we will actually reign with authority ourselves? Is that part of the teaching also? Why not? Our Lord Jesus has gone to receive a kingdom. One day that kingdom will be established on earth. He even taught us to pray. . . .**"Thy kingdom come."** There will be many exalted positions in His government. People will be needed to carry out delegated responsibilities. Surely it is in the plan of God to administer the kingdom through His agents. Even Satan's kingdom has "principalities and powers. . . .and rulers" (Eph. 6:12).

On what basis will the Lord make His appointments? **He has just told us.** The seriousness and determination with which a Christian cares for the interests of the Lord IN THIS LIFE, is the measure by which he qualifies for a job in Jesus' government. It is going to take a lot of people to run the kingdom. There will be many prime positions open to faithful servants. Those wanting a nice job with Jesus, will have to forfeit the privilege of living for themselves and compete as faithful slaves.

Compete? Certainly. How else should Jesus do it? How would you suggest He make His appointments? On the basis of favoritism? Partiality? Intelligence, persuasiveness, good looks? You know that wouldn't be fair! Since the Lord has "no respect of persons," the only fair way is to open the jobs to all who **care enough to compete** for them. And since it is a job in the future, as yet unseen, it is earned by **faith**. The competition is fair. No one has any advantage over anyone else. Since each has a mina, a man need only be faithful to invest it. His opportunity to multiply his mina is as good as any other person's in Christ.

At this writing, we have elected a new president in the United States. He has yet to take office. In the meantime he is seeking qualified people for the numerous government posts. He can't put any into office simply because they are party members. That would bring chaos to the land. The individuals must also be qualified. It is not an easy task for a new president to find the right people for the right job.

But the Lord has a way. He gives each Christian a mina, one life on earth. And while He is gone, they occupy with that mina, seeing how much they can produce for their Master. When He returns, it is already settled who gets what job. Surely we do no violence to the parable by suggesting the Lord is using it to teach His disciples the truth of His own departure and return. I expect the judgment scene to be very similar. And even the words of the Judge to ring with. . . .

> **"Well done, thou good and faithful servant. Because thou hast been faithful in a few things, I will give thee charge over many."**

Well, we still have one more parable to go. There is yet another feature to learn about our competition for a good job with Jesus.

PARABLE 4 — MATTHEW 20:1-16

Teaching: TIME (duration) is not a governing factor as the Lord measures faithfulness in a servant. **Longevity is not** an advantage in Christian work, but **willingness** is.

The parable we are about to examine declares the Lord's right to compensate His servants by His own reckoning, not theirs. Man is forced to consider TIME when computing the pay of an employee, but not the Lord. When we use the word faithfulness, we picture someone on the job a long time. But the Lord doesn't. He has His own criteria for measuring a servant's faithfulness. Just exactly what God's **faithfulness yardstick** is really like, we don't know. But that He is **not obligated** to reckon TIME as a determining factor, is clear from this parable.

Again we have a wealthy landowner. He goes to the labor market early in the morning to hire laborers. When he agrees with a group of them for a price of 18¢ a day, he sends them into his vineyard. About 9 a.m. he returns to the market. Finding more idle men, agrees with them for the same price. They go into his fields. He does the same at noon, again at 3 p.m. and once more at 5 o'clock. Even though it was getting late in the day, all were to receive the same wage, 18¢ in silver.

In the evening, the landowner himself went into the field. There he instructed his foreman to pay the workers, beginning with the last group hired, down to the first. As you would imagine, those hired first expected to receive more than those hired late in the day. But when they saw that they received no more than those who came into the fields at 5 p.m., they complained to the farmer. They grumbled that he wasn't fair. They had to endure the heat of the day, while the latecomers worked only a few evening hours.

But the landowner replied:

> **"Friends, have I really done you a wrong? Did you not agree with me for 18¢ a day? Is it not proper, even lawful, for me to do as I please with my own money? Or has my kindness to those men now caused you to become jealous?"** (Matt. 20:13, 15).

Those are the last words of the parable, to which the Lord Jesus **adds** a further comment:

> **"Many first ones shall be last, while many last ones shall be first!"**

That, of course, is the point of the parable. But what of the interpretation?

> **NOTE:** It should be stated that many scholars feel this parable does not easily give up its interpretation. Not a few confess great

> difficulty with it, so we will tread with as little presumption as possible. I can't help but feel though, that most difficulties arise from trying to press too many particulars from the story. Parables are poetic pictures taken from real life and used as vehicles for truths of the kingdom. It is when a person begins to particularize details, pressing every item for a meaning, that he runs into difficulty. We'll try to avoid that and be satisfied with the central truth.

The entire parable revolves around the Lord's admonition at the end of Chapter XIX. Peter had asked the Lord a mercenary question. . . .**"We, who have given up so much to follow you, what are we going to get out of it?"** Can't you hear Peter saying that? He has enough nerve. The essence of the Lord's reply is contained in the words. . . . ."Many first ones shall be last, while many last ones shall be first!" Then the Master proceeds to tell the story of the laborers in the vineyard. He uses the parable to explain what He means by that statement. So that statement is undoubtedly the key to the interpretation.

Interpretation

The Lord is not speaking to theologians, but common people. The truth, therefore, is to be sought on the surface of the story and not so buried it requires a "reading between the lines." What do we find on the surface? Men working **different time** spans, yet receiving the **same wage.** How may this be applied to the judgment of God's servants?

This parable, as do the other three, deals with God's workers and how they are rewarded. Each of the four views some aspect of the judgment, some feature as to **how** we earn our reward. This last parable brings up the matter of TIME. The others don't mention it. Obviously then, we are to learn what part TIME plays in rewarding Christians for faithful obedience during their earthly probation.

From the parable we see that WHEN a man went to work, and HOW LONG he was on the job had **no bearing** on his pay. Applied directly to the Christian, this suggests that because one man is called to serve the Lord early in life, he need not expect a greater reward than one who begins his servitude late in life. In other words, **longevity in service** is not necessarily an advantage. And **lateness into the race** is not necessarily a disadvantage. This can be comforting to people who are not saved until their later years. On the other hand, it warns the Christian who enjoys the luxury of being raised in a Christian home, that his privileges do not guarantee him a bigger reward.

> **NOTE:** One might deduce from this that a person could **wait** until late in life to begin his service. That would be fine if we had only this one parable. But the others show a servant is under obligation to squeeze the most from his one opportunity. If it comes early in life, he must begin early to live as a bondslave. This parable is dealing with WHEN the opportunity comes. If a man receives his MINA late in life, he is not penalized.

The Lord's yardstick for measuring **faithfulness** is applied to that portion of a person's life when he can be a slave, i.e. that moment the MINA is handed to him. It is graded in terms of intentions and willingness and how vigorously one prosecutes his opportunity, NOT **how long** he is on the job. It is possible, therefore, for those who find Christ late in life, to compete on an equal basis with those who have been serving Christ all their lives. Their chances for winning a good job with Jesus are just as good as those spending a lifetime on the job.

● This I take to be the central truth with regard to judgment and reward. However, it is true this parable can be interpreted **historically,** with the earliest Christians as first in the vineyard. Without question this was exactly how the Lord's words struck Peter. He would understand them as a specific answer to his question. . . .**"What do we get out of following you?"**

Being among the first to follow Jesus, did not automatically guarantee Peter superior status in the kingdom. Why? God's rewards are NOT based on WHEN a man is called. Otherwise, none in our generation could hope for a good job with Jesus. The prime positions would all be gone by now. The rewards, in order to be fair, must be based on the **quality** of one's devotion to the Master's interests, **not quantity**. While the different hours cited in the parable may be applied to different periods in church history, they apply just as fully to the different stages of a person's life and experience.

> **NOTE:** Again observe that these are workers, hence salvation is not in view here. Salvation is FREE, only rewards are earned. These men are being PAID for something THEY DO. The parable focuses on the hour of PAYOFF, the time of reward. It shows us that time in the field is not a critical factor in competing for the Christian crowns.

WAIT A MINUTE........!

Does someone protest?

"Hey! Didn't the Lord say somewhere that we are not His servants, but His friends? Isn't our relationship to Him something other than servant and Master?"

He did say something like that:

> "No longer do I call you slaves; for the slave does not know what his Master is doing; but I have called you friends, for all things that I have heard of My Father, I have made known unto you" (John 15:15).

That sounds like the Lord Jesus is cancelling the servant-Master relationship, doesn't it? But is He really? Does calling us "friends" remove our obligations to Him? Do we cease to be His servants because of this? He answers that Himself:

> **"You are My friends IF you DO what I command you"** (John 15:14).

Why, even friendship with Jesus is **based on obedience**. The more **faithful** one's obedience, the **closer** the friendship. He who would fully enjoy the privilege of presence with Christ, must humble himself deeper into His service. The shackles of slavery in Christ are the jewelry of eternity. Greatness in heaven is not measured as men measure greatness in this world. Did you know that the proudest trophies of the Apostle Paul were scars gained in the service of Christ. The peers of the New Testament proudly bear the title of servant:

JAMES....	"James, the **servant** of God and Jesus Christ" (Ja. 1:1)
PETER....	"Simon Peter, a **servant** and apostle of Jesus Christ" (2 Pet. 1:1)
JOHN.....	"The revelation of Jesus Christ.. unto His **servant John"** (Rev. 1:1)
JUDE.....	"Jude, the **servant of Jesus Christ."** (Vs. 1)
PAUL.....	"Paul, a **servant** of Jesus Christ, called to be an Apostle" (Rom. 1:1)

AND THAT'S NOT ALL....

Every Christian is CALLED to be a servant of the Lord. The Master means for His people to **find their happiness** serving Him. Christian slavery is a joy-breeder. Spiritual delight is the by-product of obedience. Without submission as a slave, no man can be truly happy in Christ. It is a spiritual impossibility. Here's what's so awful about it....

The Christian who does not discover the joy of serving Christ in this life, will NEVER discover it.

That's frightening. Why? We are going to be the servants of the Lord **forever!** Even in heaven He will still be the Master. He remains our Master **forever and ever.** The relationship will never change. Are we not the sons of God throughout eternity? Yes, but we will also be His servants. Let's face it: if we don't learn the JOY of serving the Lord Jesus NOW — **we never will.**

A Question . . .
. . . Crowns?

"Brother Lovett, in the earlier chapters you referred to the crowns as awards. Are the crowns of the New Testament given to Christians or do we have to earn them?"

The New Testament speaks of five crowns of the Christian and they are clearly **rewards**. I did not stop to give an exposition of the crowns earlier.

HERE'S THE LIST:

1. The crown of righteousness (2 Tim. 4:8).
2. The crown of life (Rev. 2:10).
3. The imperishable crown (1 Cor. 9:25).
4. The crown of rejoicing (Phil. 4:1).
5. The crown of glory (1 Peter 5:4).

When I say "crown," what comes to mind? You think of a jeweled head piece don't you? Maybe you see someone on a throne, his kingship symbolized by a diadem on his head? Or do you picture the royal crown in the tower of London? There is a particular Greek word for such a crown — DIADEMA. It is from this that we get our word, "diadem." It is an IMPERIAL crown. The New Testament NEVER uses this word to speak of the Christian's crown.

The Christian's crown is NOT a diadem. It is NOT an imperial crown. Yet this is what the average person pictures when the word is mentioned. We have heard about the "crowned heads" of Europe. Television has let us see a queen wearing the Imperial Crown of the British Empire. It symbolizes her position. But she did not EARN it. She inherited it. She acquired it as a birthright. The child of God, on the other hand, does NOT INHERIT any crown. He **earns** his. Therefore a different Greek word is used to speak of the Christian's crown.

The Greek for the Christian's crown is STEPHANOS. Every New Testament reference to the Christian's crown is — **"Stephanos."** This word in Greek means an EARNED **reward** or **recompense.** Sometimes the same word is used to speak of an employee's pay. That's a far cry from the idea of a royal diadem, isn't it? When a man of the first century came to Christ, he learned that he could earn a STEPHANOS. And he knew exactly what it meant. His familiarity with the Greek games made that word an instant revelation to him. He knew at once there was something to be WON in Christ.

THE GREEK GAMES.

The word "stephanos" was common throughout the Roman Empire because of the Greek games. They were the outstanding sports spectacular of that day. Akin to what we call the "International Olympics," they dominated the entertainment field of the first century. From peasant to Ceasar, everyone was interested in them. This is why the Apostle Paul used them so often as background for his teaching. Peter and John also found them useful for illustrating Christian truths.

The language of the Roman Empire was **not latin,** but GREEK. Greek was the universal language. Therefore it was the language of the games. When a new Christian found his faith expressed in words taken from the games, the meaning was precise and unmistakable. A truth clothed in this figure was crystal clear. The Christian saw at once how his new life in Christ was a CONTEST.

He understood the fantastic exertion required for progress in spiritual things. He felt himself in competition, striving for mastery. He was in a race, reaching for a prize at the end of the course. Had you and I been living in those days, we would have gained more than the meaning of the word. We would have also felt the passion and excitement that went with it. Our beings would have sensed the electrification and animation of competition in Christ. Two thousand years later, those words are simply items of biblical research.

Listen to Paul now that I have told you of these words. See if they don't carry stimulation:

> **"Do you remember how, on a racing track, every competitor runs, but only one can win the prize? Well, you ought to run with your minds fixed on winning the prize! Every competitor in the games goes into serious training. Athletes will take tremendous pains—for a fading crown of leaves. But our contest is for an eternal crown that will never fade"** (1 Cor. 9:24, 25 J. B. Phillips Trans.).

Here Paul describes the Christian life as serious competition. He asks us to think of ourselves as running in a race where only one can win. Of course many win in Christ, but he wants us to RUN (compete) as if there were only one prize.

Imagine those Greek contestants. They train for a minimum of ten months prior to the games. During that time they denied themselves many good things otherwise proper. They forfeited confections and love-making, lived on sparse food and exercised faithfully in all kinds of weather. The apostle wants us to feel the desperate efforts of these athletes. Then to see ourselves striving **just as hard** to win the prize in Christ. He didn't intend for his words to be Sunday school lessons and interesting sermon material. He meant for them to be telegrams announcing an emergency.

Paul expects Christians to become equally determined in making Christ the absolute Master of their lives. Not only straining in their tasks, but denying themselves many of the good things of this life. His illustrative use of the Greek games was not only to provide clearer teaching. He sought to communicate the heat and desperation of all-out competition in Christ. He means for his readers to become contestants — **literally**.

In the Greek games, the judges took their places on an elevated stand called the BEMA. Fix that word in your mind. You'll understand why in a moment. From the BEMA, the **"Umpire"** could watch the runners. As each **event** closed, he summoned the contestants before him. They lined up to receive their rewards. Can you see them? They are breathing heavily. Their bodies still tremble, wet with perspiration. As their names are called, each steps forward. The judge leans over and places a wreath of oak leaves on the victor's brow. That same wreath is the present day symbol of our modern Olympics.

In Greek, that word BEMA means — **the judges stand.** It is the very same word Paul uses for the Judgment Seat of Christ. **"We must all appear before the BEMA of Christ,"** says Paul (2 Cor. 5:10). The reason I ask you to keep it in mind, is because it is set against the sweaty, straining, competitive background of the Greek games. That's how Paul wants us to picture our judgment. It is not a matter of accepting gifts, but of being rewarded while still huffing and puffing as we come directly from the competition.

So don't see yourself standing before God's judgment bar as a nice, goody little Christian, who gets a crown on his head because he has been wise enough to accept God's free gift in Christ. The BEMA is not a place for handing out gifts. There is NO reward for accepting gifts. See yourself as still perspiring and panting, and what you receive is a reward for winning in competition. **Christianity is a contest**. Every one of the awards is based on competition. That is why the Judgment Seat is called the BEMA. Along with that word, keep in mind those two Greek words for crowns:

DIADEMA. . . . . the imperial crown. STEPHANOS . . . . . the competition crown. The former is INHERITED, the latter — EARNED. The imperial crown is **never** used in connection with the Christian. Only **competition** crowns are presented to the servants of Christ. This means they are for **competitors only**. Spectators are never crowned. Therefore spectators in Christianity will NOT be crowned either. All five crowns of the New Testament are reserved for those who **earn** them.

The Salvation Package*

1. **ETERNAL LIFE.** This comes as the gift of God (Rom. 6:23). But what do we receive exactly? A substance added to our souls which makes it possible for us to live forever? No. **Every** soul is designed to live forever someplace. That comes with being the "image of God." Bodies, of course, were NOT designed for eternity, nothing physical is eternal (2 Cor. 4:18). God does not have to add anything to our souls to extend human existence. All men exist eternally whether in heaven or hell. Eternal life has NOTHING TO DO WITH LONGEVITY. It is a STATE or CONDITION, even more precisely a UNION. It is the name given to that kind of life which RESULTS from JOINING an eternal man to the eternal God.

> **HINT:** Think of marriage. We take a man and join him to a woman. We refer to them as being married. Nothing has actually happened to either of them, yet they are enjoying married life. Married life is not something new added to the soul of either partner, it is the UNION of the two. Similarly, the joining of a man to God is called **Eternal Life.** Those in heaven will know the blessedness of marriage to God, those in hell will know the agony of death—eternal union with Satan. The key word is UNION.

We know little about life in the spirit, but we can be sure this UNION (eternal life) brings SATISFACTION. That is what souls ache for. Perhaps the closest thing which approximates it is **marital intimacy.** In heaven we will enjoy something not possible on earth—TOTAL INTIMACY. Our souls will be satisfied by Christ. Earthly intimacy is but a figure. Surely the intimacy of spirit-to-spirit will surpass anything we can know body-to-body. Fix the truth in your memory, by thinking of Eternal Life as married-life, married to Christ. This was how the Apostle Paul pictured it. **"I have betrothed you to Christ"** (2 Cor. 11:2, Eph. 5:32).

2. **SONSHIP.** When we are saved we become the SONS of God by birth. There is no human process which can accomplish this. The Seed which produces our spiritual birth comes from above (John 3:3). A spiritual conception occurs which is NOT simply religious THEORY, but a definite pregnancy. It is by this means that we acquire the divine nature. The second birth finds us SIRED by the Holy Spirit. **But see how this determines only WHO WE ARE, not what we DO.**

---

*Explanation of the salvation package mentioned on page 17.

OBSERVE. A woman has two sons. One turns out to be a fine, successful citizen. The other goes to prison for life. Yet, is the one in jail any less her son? No. He is still her boy even though he invested his life differently. Being good or bad doesn't affect sonship. So with the sons of God. Some grow to become lovely in the Lord, investing all in Him. Others despise their privileges, throwing away the opportunity of this life. Yet both are His. Their differences will show up at the Judgment where they will be evaluated and recompensed according to the Judge's appraisal.

3. **RIGHTEOUSNESS.** The instant we are saved, we are clothed about with a ROBE OF RIGHTEOUSNESS. This is the new nature. It was typified by Israel's high priest and his glorious robe. Within such a robe (nature) sinners can be comfortable in the presence of a Holy God. Obviously such a robe cannot be produced by sinful men. It was produced by the SINLESS Son of God and GIVEN to us at salvation. By this, He did for us what no man can do for himself. Since this ROBE is real, it cannot come by way of a decree from any religious group or body. It is not theological, **but actual.** We literally partake of the divine nature (2 Peter 1:4).

NOTE: The Christian has two kinds of righteousness. At salvation, he is provided with the ROBE which grants him **instantaneous righteousness.** However, inside that robe, the man himself is expected to advance progressively into the likeness of the Lord (2 Cor. 3:18). The personal righteousness of an individual may be referred to as **progressive righteousness.** It should be distinguished from the **instantaneous righteousness** which is his upon receipt of the new nature (robe). The robe is WORN, the righteousness of man inside **DEVELOPS.** It is important to separate these two kinds, for one is given to us by Christ as part of the salvation package. The other we develop as enabled by the Holy Spirit.

4. **FORGIVENESS.** I owe you five dollars. I don't pay. You elect to forgive my debt. Who pays? You do. Your five dollars are gone. The one who forgives, pays. If we are forgiven the guilt of our sin, someone still must pay the penalty. Jesus did. He took upon Himself the total guilt of all sin. He paid the penalty for ALL sin. Forgiveness comes to men as they **personally confess** their sin and **receive** forgiveness as individuals. Confession is something **man does.** The act of forgiving, **God does.** Were God not to forgive, it would be an act of unfaithfulness on His part since Jesus has **already** paid the penalty. But the Word says "He is faithful" to forgive (1 John 1:9). Since the penalty has been paid, forgiveness comes as a part of the salvation package.

5. **THE HOLY SPIRIT.** At salvation the Holy Spirit comes (is given) to indwell the believer. He performs a number of functions: (1) He serves as a seal, legally securing God's property. (2) He is a "down-payment" in kind, providing even now a sample of the presence of God we will know in heaven. (3) He witnesses to our own spirits that we belong to God. (4) He certifies truth so that we are not dependent on men to validate what is of God. (5) His power makes possible a holy life, and the performing of tasks assigned to us as servants of the Lord. (6) He unites all true believers into one body, the church. (7) He coaches and prompts Christians to press toward maturity in Christ. The Spirit, Himself, is a gift. He is part of the salvation package.

6. **AUTHORITY.** When we receive Christ, we receive a commission or job. We are expected to perform it as servants of the Lord. A good leader does not delegate responsibility without also granting the authority to carry it out. In the salvation package we have received the right to speak to people in the Name of the Lord. His Spirit backs our words so that people accept their authority and respond to the truth.

> **NOTE.** This authority extends to citizens of the spirit-world as well as the physical world. Since the work assigned to God's servants meets with satanic opposition, authority over Satan must be included within the commission. Christian work is crippled, if not futile, without the exercise of this authority. The devil has a wile which clouds the truth of our authority over him. It is the "safe in Christ" wile, which suggests there is automatic armor for Christians. Of course, there is none, hence the Apostle Paul says, "Put it on" (Eph. 6:11). The moment one begins to USE this authority, the truth of James 4:7 becomes operative . . . "Resist the devil and he will flee from you." Resist him not, and he won't!

7. **INHERITANCE.** The Lord Jesus has an inheritance coming. He invites us to share it as "joint-heirs" (Rom. 8:17). For Jesus to inherit from HIS **Father,** means He does so in the ROLE of SON. What does Jesus inherit? The Kingdom. This is why He says, "Come ye blessed of My Father and inherit the kingdom prepared for you . . ." (Matt. 25:34). That "Come Ye . . ." is our invitation. We receive it when we are saved. Therefore we expect to see the Lord in His kingdom. He even instructed us to pray for it — "Thy kingdom come. . . ." The kingdom features the APPEARANCE of Jesus, once more on earth and REIGNING in glory. We are to share this with Him (Col. 3:4). As "joint-heirs" of this kingdom, we will also be revealed with Him, covered with His glory. Every Christian will participate in this whether he is alive at the coming of Christ or not. Those who have died in Christ, God will "bring with Him" (1 Thess. 4:14).

Brother Lovett was saved through his "accidental" attendance at a minister's conference where he eavesdropped the conversation of a group of nationally known Christian leaders. There he overheard a discussion on the mechanics of salvation. For years he had been under conviction, yet no one troubled to introduce him to Christ. Armed with the necessary insight for the salvation experience, he hurried home to share it with his wife, Marjorie.

Together they knelt and invited Christ to come into their hearts. This delayed salvation experience accounts for his burden to do away with the vague and shadowy notions of Christianity and present the truths of God's Word man to man.

A graduate of California Baptist Theological Seminary, he holds the M.A. and B.D. degrees conferred Magna Cum Laude. He has completed graduate work in Psychology at Los Angeles State College and holds an honorary doctorate from the Protestant Episcopal University in London. He is a retired Air Force Chaplain with the rank of Lt. Colonel.

Pastor Lovett is the author of the books and tools produced by Personal Christianity. Able to express the profound things of God in simple, practical language, his writings strengthen Christians the world over. The advent of his "Soul-Winning Made Easy," has drastically changed evangelism methods in America, while the anti-satan skill offered in his "Dealing with the Devil," has alerted multitudes to their authority over our enemy through Christ. Dr. Lovett's experience as an editor of the Amplified New Testament and a director of the foundation which produced it, prompted him to begin work on the Personal New Testament Commentary.

DR. LOVETT

is pastor of PC